CW01502163

A narrow lane in southern England, on one of the longest days of the year. We have been walking for hours, following the path into the valleys and then up onto the hills, into wind and light. Behind us, miles of B-roads and cycle paths, bridleways and trackways – and before us, a steep descent into a valley. For now, though, we are standing deep in the lane, deep in cover, beneath trees that lean and fold into the air. The path curves ahead, the banks lined with flowers.

We share a packet of oatcakes while looking over a map. Then we climb up the sides of the path and peer over the hedge. Acres of farmland slope away from us – glowing prisms of barley, bright slopes of grass – and intersecting these grids, and surrounding them, we can see a larger patchwork of green fields. Further off, the fields darken into woods, and beyond the woods are the hills of a distant range.

'Chaffinch,' my friend says, suddenly turning towards a tree. Then, tilting his head in another direction, then another, he names the birds around us: 'Great tit, blackcap, greenfinch, wren.' We listen in the stillness of the noonday heat, and at one point we hear eight songs around us, eight distinctive calls.

'Bullfinch?' I ask, when a new bird starts up.

'Greenfinch,' he says. 'Listen to the wheeze in the middle of the call. Sounds like a whisky-drinking jazz singer. Bullfinch is a rusty gate.'

'OK, got it. Greenfinch, jazz. Bullfinch, gate.'

'Exactly.'

We come to the end of the lane and step into a narrow field. Yellowhammers scatter before us, emerging from the hedge in volleys of light, and as we follow them into another field, overgrown with weeds and flowers, it seems as though we are walking deeper into the summer, on a day when time seems new again. More yellowhammer-blur, then a skylark striking up in the next field, dropping bright pebbles of sound, and everywhere before us the lit fuse of summer: clusters of herb robert and red campion, undergroves of knapweed and vetch, deep rows of hogweed and teasel. We cross the field, step down into another lane, and then pause to study the way: a path flanked by steep banks, the track shadowed by holly and ash.

Later that evening – after a full day of walking, and after we return to Bristol – I stop before entering my house. Across the road, three birds are singing deep in greenery, in late summer light. A gust of wind shakes the trees,

LATE
LIGHT

LATE LIGHT

MICHAEL MALAY

**MANILLA
PRESS**

First published in the UK by Manilla Press
an imprint of Bonnier Books UK
4th Floor, Victoria House
Bloomsbury Square
London, England, WC1B 4DA
Owned by Bonnier Books
Sveavägen 56, Stockholm, Sweden

facebook.com/bonnierbooksuk/
twitter.com/bonnierbooksuk

Hardback – 9781786581419
Ebook – 9781786581426
Audio – 9781786581433

All rights reserved. No part of the publication may be reproduced,
stored in a retrieval system, transmitted or circulated in any form or
by any means, electronic, mechanical, photocopying, recording or
otherwise, without prior permission in writing of the publisher.

A CIP catalogue of this book is available from the British Library.

Cover designed by © Andy Lovell, 2023
Typeset by IDSUK (Data Connection) Ltd
Printed and bound by Clays Ltd, Elcograf S.p.A

1 3 5 7 9 10 8 6 4 2

Copyright © Michael Malay, 2023

Michael Malay has asserted his moral right to be identified as the author of
this Work in accordance with the Copyright, Designs and Patents Act 1988.

Every reasonable effort has been made to trace copyright holders of
material reproduced in this book, but if any have been inadvertently
overlooked the publishers would be glad to hear from them.

Manilla Press is an imprint of Bonnier Books UK
www.bonnierbooks.co.uk

For Catherine and Clara

Contents

'Life is roomy yet, and the odds unbounded.' Thomas Hardy

'It gets late early out there.' Yogi Berra

LATE LIGHT

swirling the branches like oversize pom-poms, and for a moment the songs are lost. But when the wind dies the notes become present again, and the songs unreel themselves into the listening air. Yes, there they are: *blackbird, chaffinch, wren.*

*   *   *

The lanes and the trackways; the narrow paths gleaming after rain, and the wide roads baking under summer heat; and other paths, quieter ones, that seemed like portals into other realms: valleys, orchards, combes. For a long time these paths and roads were new to me. Also the birds that sang in the hedges and the flowers that grew by the lanes. At first, being a stranger here, I did not know the names for things, and so could not place myself in the landscape. I saw the valleys and the ancient walls and the strange trees in the woods – trees with many-fingered branches growing out of stumps, a quiver of arrows – but it was months before I understood that these were coppiced trees, coppiced hazel to be precise, and longer still before I learned terms such as 'combe' or 'drystone wall'.

I saw other things, equally strange. Medieval streets of extraordinary crookedness, laid with stones called 'cobbles'. The barrel-shaped roof of Bristol's central train station, larger than any roof I had seen. And the ruins of a church in the city centre, parts of which remained after having been bombed during the Second World War. Then there were the pubs which, with their misshapen crossbeams and warped door-frames, seemed to be sinking into the ground, but which the locals entered without a second glance. Some pubs carried a sign that said 'free house' or 'public house', and almost all were decorated with strange insignia: a portcullis, a cockerel, a lion, a crown.

In the north of the city, at the top of a steep hill, was a grassland inexplicably called 'The Downs' and below the grassland was a river called the Avon. The river made its way through a gorge and emptied out into the Bristol Channel, and if you wanted to you could walk across the Severn Bridge into Wales, another country. The water separating England and Wales was darkly coloured, gun-metal grey or greyish blue, and once, when crossing the bridge, I noticed a large creature swimming beneath the estuary's surface, perhaps a seal or a porpoise.

I would sometimes cycle into the countryside, along the small roads that connected Bristol to nearby towns and villages. And it was during those trips that I saw my first English cottages. The houses were basic in their design – a garden, a wooden door, a chimney – and in their simplicity seemed to me like drawings from a child's picture book, a fantasy of the simple life. Roses grew in the gardens, alongside daffodils and other flowers I recognised from books and films. Many of the plants, however, were new to me, and although I would later learn their names – foxglove, wisteria, delphinium – they were like dream flowers at first, not quite real. In certain villages, too, I noticed that some cottages were fitted with strange windows, large bulbous protrusions that looked like mistakes. At some point, I would learn that this was a style known as 'crown glass', and that such windows had once been common in England. In those early days, though, all I could see were the odd ripples in the glass.

The strangeness would disappear in time – the strangeness of new English words and my sense of not belonging to the landscape. And soon I would use the terms others were using, would begin to speak of 'A' roads and 'B' roads, 'bridleways', 'stiles' and 'kissing gates'. When I think back to those first months, though, all I remember is that feeling of oddity, of not being able to make sense of what I saw. I was a young man when I came to England, twenty-one years old, and yet during those early weeks, and because of my difficulty in understanding certain accents, or of making myself understood, some of my first interactions were reduced to basic gestures or simple words, as though I had become a child again.

There was something else as well, a deeper discomfort. During those first months, I sometimes had the sense that there were two conversations happening at once – the things that were being said and the subtext beneath those words. So that, alongside the strangeness of arrival – alongside those cottages and their gardens, the drystone walls and the coppiced trees – there was the difficulty of social encounters, the confusion of not knowing the code. 'I thought he was rather earnest', someone once said to me, while discussing a film we had just watched. He was describing the main actor in the film, and it was only years later, after I had heard a similar remark from someone else, that I realised 'earnest' was not a word of praise, as I had first understood it, but a criticism, a way of expressing disapproval. If you were rather earnest, you were over-bearing, too frank with your emotions. The actor was American. I was beginning to pick up the code.

I look out from my office in Bristol – it is a summer day, the ash trees are stirring in light – and I think back to those weeks and months when I first came to England. What were those experiences like, those first encounters with English things and places, and with the accents and weather of Bristol? At times, I remember feeling self-conscious, aware of my out-of-placeness in the countryside and in social settings. But I also remember astonishment at the things I experienced. Astonishment at the crooked medieval streets, for example, or the ringing of the cathedral bells, so unlike the calls to prayer I grew up with in Indonesia, and which, though pealing from a mile away, would float through my open window and fill the room with their sound. Above all, though, I remember the light. The lingering light of my first summer in England, and my amazement at that light.

I could not believe the days could last so long. In Jakarta, where I lived until I was ten, the nights came on swiftly – the sun would set and you would be in the dark – and it was much the same in Australia, where I lived until I was twenty. But in England the hills would hold the light for hours, as though the sun had become mechanically stuck in its descent – no longer in view and yet close enough to light everything up: the valleys, the sky, the paths. I loved the light of those long evenings and the mood of those suspended hours; and I liked the experience of walking deep into blueness. And after that first year, and after those long evenings started to dwindle, I began to understand what it meant to long for the summer to return – that sense of waiting for a season. And the summers did return: first one, then two, until more than a decade of such summers had passed for me in England.

* * *

As the years go by, it becomes harder to remember those first days and the process by which strange things became familiar and known. Difficult also to remember that period of in-betweenness, when my original sense of a word or phrase came into contact with how the terms were being used by others. In childhood, I had come across the word 'bramble' in a book by Roald Dahl and had formed a clear picture of what it meant: an impenetrable thicket, a place you could not pass. But when I came to England, I learned that you could also find blackberries on brambles and that people went blackberrying in the summer. There were other words that I had to reconsider – 'hawthorn', 'meadow', 'uplands' – terms that had conjured strong images for me as a boy, but which, after encountering them in England, I realised meant slightly different things for the people who were using them.

Even Bristol, the city to which I had come as a postgraduate student, had been a word from a book. When I was twelve or thirteen, the stepfather of a friend, an Englishman, began sharing parts of his library with me. He had grown up in Liverpool in the 1950s, and after noticing my interest in reading began to introduce me to the stories of his own childhood: *Peter Rabbit*, *The Wind in the Willows*, *The Lord of the Rings*. He also gave me a book about a man named Biggles, a fighter pilot for the British RAF, and this pilot, whose full name was actually James Bigglesworth, would sometimes take to the air in a plane called the *Bristol Fighter*. Long before I was aware of Bristol as the name of a city, then, I first knew it as the name of an aeroplane, and it was only much later, when I became a student in England, that I learned that 'Bristol', which derives from 'Brycgstow', once meant the 'place of the bridge'.

Over the years, the word Bristol has accrued many more meanings for me – the place where I heard dubstep for the first time, where I split my head open during a football match, where I found love and lost love, and where I eventually got married. Even today, though, a faint echo of that child's view persists in the centre of that word. 'Bristol': the name of a plane in a book; a synonym for adventure and danger.

As for those words I picked up in England – 'hedgerows', 'downs', 'combes' – they carry no echoes of childhood for me and have only English associations. And though these words are familiar now, I can still remember how odd they were during the enigma of arrival. They were words from a foreign place, strange on the tongue and in the ear, and sometimes, when I find myself thinking about those first months, something of their original jolt returns to me, since this was a time when language felt fresh again and when so much was new and untested. 'Hedgerow': a vertical garden, a refuge for birds. 'Downs': a green space in north Bristol, but also a term for open chalk hills. 'Combe': a little hollow or valley. There was that difficulty of not knowing the codes – the grammar of social life in Britain – but beneath those things, and stronger than them, was the experience of stepping into the marvellous. The long blue evenings of an English summer. The flowers growing along the banks of a narrow lane. And the birds singing from tree to tree, or chimney to chimney – an unbroken line of song that seemed to connect Bristol with the fields of Somerset, Gloucestershire and beyond.

* * *

'Pack light,' Dad had said, in the weeks before I left home. It was 2008, the year I left Australia to study in England, and I followed his advice by travelling with one suitcase, a half-size guitar, and a winter coat my mother had bought from a charity store in Brisbane and which, having learned that it sometimes snowed in Bristol, she had lined with an extra layer of fleece. They both thought I'd be back within a year, and so did I, though in the end six years would pass before I eventually returned, by which point everything had changed. During my time abroad, Mom had returned to her hometown in Indonesia, Dad to his in America (the divorce was, thankfully, amicable) and later the family house was sold. And then – it happened so suddenly, so randomly – Dad died in an accident. I did not cry at his funeral in Illinois, but a year later, when I went back to Australia, and after I spent a few days driving to the places he had taken me as a boy, the tears came and did not stop. It was the view that did it: I was by the shop where he used to buy fish and chips.

Gone, all of it gone, and yet, in the years before they parted ways, and whenever I phoned them, my parents seemed OK about their son who never returned home. 'As long as you're happy out there,' Mom would say, or 'As long as you know what you're doing,' Dad would sometimes add. In truth, I had no idea what I was doing, but I suppose I was what my mother wanted me to be. My life in England was new, enriching and fun, and, in the self-absorbed way of someone in his early twenties, I hardly thought about home or my parents during that first year. England, which had once been mysterious to me, was now the only important thing, while Australia, the place I had known as home, seemed unreal and far away.

At university, where I was studying English literature, I was also encountering people unlike any I had met before. I spent my teens on the Gold Coast, in south-east Queensland, and at school the main obsessions of my classmates were cricket, rugby, surfing and cars, interests which I partly shared, but which also felt cleaved off from what I was reading about in books, the stuff that really excited me. When I came to England, a world that had formerly been private – one of books and ideas and fictional characters – suddenly became communal. I was in a foreign country, but among other people who loved the same things.

Our classes took place along Woodland Road, not far from the city centre. I came to know the road well that first year – the walls with their missing stones, the sequence of trees as you walked towards the library – and it was there, during conversations before or after seminars, that I met people who would become lifelong friends. There was Steven, a beer-guzzling student of Russian literature; Jack, a gentle scholar of Buddhism; Peter, a baseball-obsessed historian studying medieval peasantry; and Michaela, a Slovakian student from the Drama department, who, just like me, had recently arrived in England.

As it happened, some of these friends were naturalists – Jack was a botanist, Steven an expert on birds – and it was thanks to them that I began to learn the names for things. We would take long walks around Bristol or in the countryside, and without it ever being their intention, they

13

helped to place me in the landscape. 'Aspens,' I would say after Jack, when a breeze lit up a row of silvery trees. Or, standing with Steven on some country lane, I would learn to distinguish the song of a blackbird from a robin, or a chiffchaff from a chaffinch. They also taught me other things: the usefulness of certain herbs – yarrow for toothaches, plantain for stings – the names of the berries in the hedges – blackberry, hawthorn, sloe – and how to brew cider in plastic bottles (alcohol content unknown; effects: exuberance and memory loss).

Through them, I also became acquainted with English songs, traditions, ways of seeing. Thanks to his photo-graphic memory, Peter had an astonishing recall for history, and whenever he wasn't talking about baseball, his first and most enduring love, he would tell me about farming traditions in England, or recite the lyrics of old folk songs, or describe important transformations in the country's past. During our walks, he would also touch his baseball cap whenever we saw a magpie, and when I finally asked him what he meant by this, he told me that it was a reflex from childhood, and that the magpie was the bird of which he was most wary. He said this without any irony or self-consciousness, something that struck me at the time; and now, whenever I pass a magpie, I cannot help but think of Peter's instinctive touching of his cap, nor the rhyme he would sometimes repeat: *five for silver, six for gold*.

During that first year, I also began filling notebooks with words gleaned from books and friends; terms like 'heath', 'upland' and 'fen', or 'furze', 'hart's tongue' and 'goose-grass', or 'Icknield Way' and 'Fosse Way'. I liked gathering these words. They were like pebbles found on a beach, shapely and good to hold, and some opened strange vistas onto the past. When I learned that Bredon Hill contained three hills in one, for example – 'bre' comes from the Celtic term for hill, while 'don' is the Old English word – I began to realise how deep some of these names went, and how much the passage of time had complicated their roots.

There were other words, too: simple ones that altered how I saw the landscapes around me. When I learned to identify rowan and ash, for example, and to meet them during my walks, I also began to notice the trees that grew beside them, which became conspicuous for not being the ones I knew. In turn, learning about these trees introduced me to others, which drew my attention to others still. Season by season, and walk by walk, I was learning that the fields were full of words and that the words were full of fields, and that, if you wanted a small part of this abundance, all you had to do was look.

And it was Michaela, my Slovakian friend, with whom I could discuss these things and talk about the migrant's experience of England. We would meet at a cafe called Channings, a name we both found faintly exotic – like Wimbledon, or Salisbury, or the Cotswolds – and talk about the strange customs of our new country, or about the things we were missing from home. I would tell Michaela about my childhood in Indonesia and Australia, and she would tell me about her life in Slovakia: long summers at her grandmother's house in the countryside, her childhood in Bratislava, honey from the Carpathian Mountains. That was the autumn of 2009, a year into my life in Britain.

A new spring came and went, a tide of white blossom and warming light. Then the summer arrived and there were more blue nights. And as these things happened – as acorns grew fat with sunlight, and as elderberries grew secretive and dark – something in me shifted, and in ways I still do not fully understand. Simply put, I realised that I did not have to go back home, because home had lost its grip on me. I also understood something else: that I could – and that I would – stay on in England. It was a slightly bewildering feeling, like being lost on some foreign road, and yet it felt liberating too, because that road could take me anywhere. I could just keep walking, following the paths as they opened up before me.

And as the years passed – years during which Michaela returned to Slovakia, Peter to Oxfordshire, and Steven moved to Wales, and during which I became a teacher at the university where I had enrolled as a student – I found myself becoming accustomed to rhythms that were once foreign, and to words and experiences that were never mine: the taste of bitter ale, the return of swifts in late spring, and the names for places – 'Coombe Dingle', 'Broadmead', 'Shirehampton' – words I came to use with increasing ease. I began to feel a kind of closeness to these things, too, if only because they had begun to possess me in some way. 'And that?' my sister once asked me, when she visited England for the first time. 'Ash,' I would say, before repeating a description I had heard many years ago. 'You can tell by how the trunk forks into the air, and by the way the branches hold their seeds in clusters.'

I was beginning to feel at home, or, if not exactly at home, then at least no longer a stranger to these shores.

* * *

When I look back to that first year in England, two other moments stand out in memory for me. The first was the discovery of Gerard Manley Hopkins, whose poetry came to obsess me for years, and the second was joining a reading group devoted to British politics. Both expanded the world for me, by letting in new kinds of information, new kinds of light; and although both interests ran parallel for a long time, not converging until recently, I see now how central they have been to the weave of my life in England.

I first read Hopkins in the garden of the house I was lodging in. It was a summer day, I had a mug of milky tea beside me, and after reading his poem 'The Windhover', about a kestrel rebuffing the 'big wind' with its own 'hurl and gliding', I remember looking up from the page to a slightly altered world. Not everything in the poem made sense, and it took many readings before I felt I could grasp it. Yet the poem passed through me like a wave, stirring up the strangest images in my mind even as it brought a kind of clarity in its wake. I had no idea that poetry could do what Hopkins made it do – that it could take off your head, crack open your heart – and I wanted more of it.

What Hopkins offered was another way of looking. He helped you see what he called 'inscape' – that sum of elements and graceful inner tensions that make a thing distinctively *that* thing. According to Hopkins, inscape is what you see when the being of a thing leaps out at you, so that you are no longer in the company of an object or an 'it' but a living presence. And he found it everywhere: in blue-bell flowers brightening the air, in the colour-shimmer of a trout's skin under a bridge, and in the breaking folds of a wave down-curling into itself. In his poems, everything sang the song of itself in distinctive ways, declaring its being in a style nothing else could replicate or approach.

After reading Hopkins' poetry, I became interested in how other poets wrote about animals – a subject that formed the heart of a doctoral thesis I began in Bristol. 'What?' my sister said, sincerely astonished. 'That's actually a *thing*?' Other members of my family were equally surprised. As a teenager, I had never shown any real interest in the natural world, and they couldn't understand why I would start now. To me, though, the project was an extension of what I was already experiencing in England. Friends had taught me the names of birds and plants; through Hopkins I found a living language for the rich aliveness of the world, an astonished yet never cloying nor sentimental reverence for the beauty of things.

Not long after that first experience of Hopkins, I also began attending a reading group near the city centre. The meetings took place in a basement room of a small cafe, and every month we would read a book or series of articles devoted to a new topic: the origins of the British labour movement, the history of the British empire, the development of neoliberalism in the 1970s and '80s. The meetings were attended by students, bus drivers, postal workers, teachers and retirees, and sometimes, when the meetings continued past the cafe's opening times, the workers in the cafe would join us rather than booting us out. We drank lots of over-stewed tea in that basement, and later, when the discussions were over, lots of beer in the local pub.

One effect of the reading group was to make me see England again. Through our discussions, I learned about the impact of the housing crisis on their lives, the growing prevalence of zero-hours contracts, and the slow dismantling of the welfare state, and I came to see the myriad ways that political forces shaped almost every aspect of life in Britain: from what school you went to and the concentration of air pollution in your neighbourhood, to whether you were given sick leave or provided with adequate social care, to how long you lived – or how young you died. The reading group helped me make sense of other things, too: the growing number of tents appearing at the edges of Bristol's parks, erected by the city's homeless; the lengthening lines outside a soup kitchen on Stapleton Road, which I passed as I cycled home in the evenings, and the sense of powerlessness and despair many people were feeling in the early 2010s, as Britain struggled to recover from one of the worst recessions since the Second World War.

And so England, which had once been mysterious to me, was now becoming complicated. The enchantment started to fade, and I began to see what I could not during the flush of arrival: crisis, loss, transformation. I was beginning to properly arrive in England, even though by that point I had been in Bristol for more than a year. I was realising something else, too, something that became increasingly obvious the longer I worked on my PhD thesis. I was writing about the tracks animals leave in the world and in our imaginations, but the more walks I took with birdwatchers and naturalists, the more I learned how much was missing from the landscape. I would learn the name for a particular bird, for instance, a curlew or a lapwing, but later learn that it was no longer common in the UK. Or I would learn that yellowhammers were critically endangered, or that field-fares, curlews and pied flycatchers were retreating from their former ranges. The animals I was learning about from friends, or reading about in poems, were vanishing. I was discovering a world of disappearing things.

* * *

What happens to the world – to landscapes, to other animals, to us – when a species disappears? How does extinction alter the fabric of life? I began to explore these questions several years ago, when I became increasingly aware that my original sense of England, formed through the books and films I had encountered as a boy, many of which emphasised the beauty of the landscape or the continuity of the past, was an illusion. In those early days, all I could see was the charm of surfaces – the bright streams, the curving lanes, the undulating fields – and because I had been prepared to see these things, I did not think to look further. Later, when I learned that Britain was among the most 'nature-depleted' countries in the world, I started to look again. The initial charm faded, yet what appeared in its wake was a much more intricate reality, one which, though it revealed damaged and fragmented landscapes, also introduced me to a country that was much more complicated than the version of England I had carried in my mind. A haunted England, but also a more truthful one; an England in particular.

This book is the result of that renewed engagement with my adopted country. It is a book about lost and vanishing things, as well as a book about the wonder and strangeness of being alive at this time. It tells the story of four animals that are disappearing from the British Isles – eels, moths, freshwater mussels and crickets – and recounts the four years I have spent learning about them, looking for them, and talking to the people (anglers, naturalists, conservationists, biologists) who love and care for them. It is also about the ecosystems that support these creatures, as well as the distinctive regions of human culture that animals inhabit. Because we share our land-scapes with them, we also share a common reality, and our historical experience of that reality is part of what makes us human. This book is about the gift of these shared worlds and the things that are lost as they begin to unravel.

It is partly by chance that I started writing about these animals. Years ago, I came across a flyer advertising a moth-trapping course in Somerset and took it home. I missed the course that year – the leaflet was lost under a pile of papers – but when the flyer eventually resurfaced, I learned that the course was an annual event and decided to book a place. The next summer I travelled to the Quantock Hills, in west Somerset, and during a week in August, I found myself in the company of lepidopterists obsessed with creatures I knew nothing about, including Blue Underwings, Dingy Footmans and Powdered Quakers. They were strange and reclusive beings (the moths, but also some of the lepid-opterists) and many of them carried wonderful patterns and colours on their wings: white-marbled landscapes, gleaming bronzed surfaces, deep reds and dusky blues.

The other animals also came my way by chance. In a pub in London, I heard about the eel's life cycle – its migra-tion to the rivers of Europe from the Sargasso Sea, a journey which, towards the end of its life, it completes again in reverse – and soon enough I was hooked. I picked up a copy of *The Book of Eels*, Tom Fort's magisterial study of the fish, and started loitering by streams and rivers in Bristol, hoping to catch an aspect of them: glint of eye, whip of tail. I saw many interesting things during that eel-obsessed time, among them submerged tents and rubber gloves, shopping trolleys and plastic bags, but the creatures eluded me, and it was only much later, when a conservationist put me in touch with a group of anglers, that I held my first eel in my hands.

The obsessions of others have always fascinated me. I know a woman who unicycled across England in her twenties and a man who collects obscure Scandinavian heavy-metal LPs. In the past, though, I have observed these passions from a slightly bemused – and perhaps even condescending – distance, safe in the knowledge that I myself was immune to them. After those first meetings with eels and moths, however, I began to understand what such an obsession might be, and where it might lead. For it was through my interest in eels that I came to learn about the freshwater pearl mussel, and it was that connection which ultimately led me to a river in the Highlands, where a Scottish conservationist showed me how to look for the outline of gleaming shells with a glass-bottom bucket. I was learning how way leads onto way, as a Robert Frost poem has it, and how, as you travel deeper into the worlds of other animals, new and stranger doors will open for you. One of those doors led me to crickets, and that was perhaps the most important door of all, since it reminded me that the familiar and the nearby are just as fascinating as the rare and faraway, and that to make contact with the wildness of the nonhuman world all you need is your local patch.

The creatures in this book are not commonly thought of as 'charismatic species' – the name given to animals with broad popular appeal. That choice is deliberate. I wanted to write about animals who, though known to us, are also ignored, unloved or neglected in some way. I also wanted to show how, with a slightly different way of looking, we might discover enigmatic worlds in the familiar places where we live. In fact, with the exception of freshwater pearl mussels, the animals in this book are widely found in fields, rivers and woodlands. They are the exotic neighbours living close by, the marvellous minds with whom we share the ordinary.

Of course, popular species also need their defenders. They too are slipping out of the living world, for many of the same reasons that are threatening the lesser-known animals around them. But the consequence of foregrounding certain species has been to create shadow zones elsewhere. Our modes of valuing the natural world – our obsession with charisma, for example, or our fixation on beauty – has led to inequalities of recognition, which in turn have influenced what we try to conserve, and what we neglect. In this way, many animals have become the victims of both material and cultural forces: the physical destruction or contamination of their habitats, and their exclusion from circles of care.

It is for this reason that this book focuses on what might be called 'edge species', animals who exist on the margins of our attention, and who consequently struggle to find a place in our hearts. The conservation campaigns devoted to butterflies far outnumber those devoted to moths, for example, while the vast sums that go into conserving the Atlantic salmon bear no comparison with the meagre funds that support the freshwater pearl mussel, a species which, at least in Scotland, shares many of the same habitats as this charismatic fish. By emphasising creatures that are often disregarded, this book tries to redress the imbalance.

Learning about these animals has expanded my sense of this country. In order to meet them, I have had to immerse myself in landscapes both faraway and close at hand, and to see these places from their perspective. In turn, this has opened up new ways of thinking and feeling, since it has been impossible to follow these animals into their worlds without being moved and changed in some way, and without wondering, too, how we might become better neighbours to them and live with greater care and generosity in the world. Unexpectedly, these animals have also redeemed the notion of 'charisma' for me. In its usual application, the concept is exclusionary, since it foregrounds certain animals at the expense of others. Approached in a more egalitarian spirit, however, the idea of 'a charismatic species' may contain a basic truth, in the sense that the more closely you observe anything, the more singular it becomes before your eyes – the more interesting, confounding, vital, alive.

What would a world full of charismatic beings look like? It would be a miraculous place, crazily rich in its detail and almost overwhelmingly full in its aliveness. Which, as it happens, is precisely the world we are fortunate enough to inhabit – and the world we are losing.

*   *   *

A warm evening in Bristol, late in the summer. I am walking across the Downs, following a route I have walked many times before. The night is gathering, touching everything in grey-blue light, and I go right to the edge of the gorge, where I can lean against a fence and look down at the river two hundred feet below. A flock of gulls appears in the distance, tumbling in the turbulence of the wind, and then a cormorant arrows into sight, black wings beating hard against air, and not long after some blue tits scatter from nearby scrub, disturbed by something I cannot see. They move away in a dipping flight, chattering as they go.

On a clear day you can stand here and see the bluish hills of Wales to the west. And often, when visiting this place with friends, I have done what I am doing now: walk to the edge of the Downs and search for the outlines of those distant hills. Many of those friends have left now, having returned home or moved to other cities. From time to time, though, and in certain moods, I fancy that I can see them in the distance, walking on the Downs . . .

As I can see them right now, further along the path:

There is Jack, showing us the difference between cow parsley and hemlock; and there is Peter, touching his baseball cap as a magpie walks past; and now here is Michaela, telling me about a passage she has come across in a Dickens novel, a passage she found so funny that she cannot describe it without breaking down in fits of laughter; and now here is Steven, his head tilted towards the scrub, listening to the birds singing around us. They are walking and laughing and sometimes shaking their heads, no older than they were on the day we met, but seeming to recede whenever I come too near, and always out of earshot.

Their ghosts are part of these fields now, and as real to me as the clumps of hawthorn that sprawl across the Downs. And yet, as I walk here this afternoon, warmed by the memories of those days, I am also full of anxieties I have no name for, a pervasive sense of trouble. It is the anxiety of knowing that the weather is wrong (many of us can feel it in our bodies), and that we are failing badly in our care of the earth ('Everything is broken,' a friend had said earlier that year). Also the wildfires in the Arctic Circle – Siberia, Alaska, Greenland – and the thinning of the world's ice, including the loss of ice shelves the size of Manhattan. And the destruction, the insane destruction, of the animal communities with whom we share the world.

I turn for home – it is getting dark now, the last blues are leaking away – and then for some reason I think of something that Yogi Berra once said: 'It gets late early out there.' The famous catcher for the New York Yankees, Berra was describing the original Yankee Stadium and was referring to how, as daylight began to fade during a game, one side of the field, the left-hand side, would be plunged into darkness before the rest of the stadium, such that some outfielders would be in shadow while the rest stood in light. And sometimes, reading a newspaper in the morning, or listening to the radio at night, it can seem as though we have entered history's left-hand field, a place where it's become dark much too early.

But as I continue walking – now I am on the campus where I first arrived as a student – and as I think of melting ice and wildfires and the Yankee Stadium, it occurs to me how easy it is to aestheticise loss, and how what is needed is not lament (although that may sometimes have its place) but politics and attention and care. Some of the worst of the devastation can still be assuaged, and other worlds can still be imagined and built, and as long as that is the case, as long as those openings are there, then it is always too soon to leave the field. Yes, it gets late early out there, but there's still light. The innings go on.

EEL

Several years ago, I began going to a place called Severn Beach, a village in South Gloucestershire. It lies ten miles north of Bristol, at the mouth of the River Severn, and was easily reached from my home by train. At first I went every few months, but it wasn't long before I began visiting every fortnight and then every week.

The visits took place during a difficult time, when I was feeling unmoored in the world. My father had recently died, some close friends had left Bristol, and then I had parted ways with a long-term girlfriend. My UK visa was also about to expire, and although I had been planning to renew it, I was now feeling unsure. Perhaps it was time to move on from Bristol, I thought, or even leave England altogether. For something else was happening, too, no doubt precipitated by recent events: I was feeling homesick. And not just homesick, but adrift and lonely and lost in a way I had never felt before. Since leaving Australia, I had been in the grip of wanderlust, happy to follow the paths as they appeared before me. During those hard months, though, I began to long for childhood landscapes, for remembered things and known vistas. I wanted to go back.

I could not understand why at the time, but these anxieties would partly subside whenever I came to Severn Beach. I would board the train at Lawrence Hill, not far from where I live in east Bristol, and watch as streets and houses gave way to factories and industrial estates, before the landscape became a soft and blurry region of estuary and saltmarsh. Then I would walk a few miles along the estuary, usually as far as Aust or Oldbury-upon-Severn, although sometimes I would go further, staying out late into the evening. 'Why?' friends later asked, when they noticed how much time I was spending there, and yet how could I explain what I did not understand myself? All I knew was that, whenever I went to Severn Beach, a lightness would return to my body, which was the lightness of knowing that, for a moment, I was rightly placed in the world.

Not far from the train station, you will find a ramp at the end of the main road. Climb it. This is the seawall of Severn Beach, and as you walk up you are often scoured by wind, which sweeps past in long relentless streams or short manic bursts. You are at one of the edges of England, meeting the winds as they arrive from the Atlantic, and before you is the rocky, muddy, salty, light-filled world of the Severn Estuary. Big sky, big water. Miles of mud.

Nothing is at rest here, even when the place seems still. At high tide, water comes barrelling up the estuary, squeezed into a roiling force by the narrowing banks of the Bristol Channel, and as the tide goes out, islands of mud begin to emerge from the water – small outcrops that gradually turn into vast mudflats. It is a reliably smelly place – the sulphurous mud and rotting seaweed get right up your nose – but it is also full of glorious sleights of hand. When the sun burnishes the water with the right sheen, the sheen of hammered gold, or of mackerel shoals turning beneath the sun, the estuary can look strangely insubstantial, less estuary than floating plane of light. Then the estuary seems to levitate above the seafloor, as if, at this time of light-dazzle, water were exempt from the laws governing mass. Always, though, the estuary's pong brings you back to earth, rubbing salt and mud into your visions of another world.

I did not always like it. Years before I became a regular visitor, I had come to Severn Beach on a whim, curious to see what lay at the end of the train line. This was in 2008, the year I first arrived in Bristol, and I remember feeling disappointed by what I saw: the turbid water of the estuary, the monotony of the saltmarsh, the endless mud. There was no place to swim, no sand to sift through your fingers, and nothing I could recognise as 'beach'. I don't think I stayed very long.

But if I did not care for this estuary when I first came, I now feel drawn to it. I like to see what happens here: the locals walking along the seawall, the birds banking in the freedom of the air, and the island of Flat Holm in the distance, a bar of gold laid across the estuary. In recent years, I have also been coming for what I cannot see. Every spring, this is where juvenile eels appear in their millions, newly arrived from the Atlantic Ocean, and every autumn, this is where adult eels depart in their thousands, on their way back to the Sargasso Sea. And in between these comings and goings there are eels who, having migrated here many years ago, and having been content to go no further upstream, have made this estuary their home. Somehow, despite the churn of forces passing through this place – billions of litres of water, carrying millions of tonnes of silt – the eels have found a way of staying put, and I often think of them there, coiling and uncoiling in the dark, their eyes riveted to the moon.

'There are tides in the body,' Virginia Woolf writes, hidden urgings and gravitational forces. Not all of them make sense, at least to our rational minds. As a teenager growing up in Queensland, I lived by a large body of water on the Gold Coast, a shallow estuary that extended for twelve miles and which I would explore in my family's 'tinny', a small aluminium boat with a six-horsepower engine. I spent most of my weekends on the estuary, usually alone, but sometimes with my dad and my siblings. And much later in my life, after having lived in England for more than five years, and after I became a frequent visitor to Severn Beach, it suddenly made sense. I was coming here for the estuary itself, for the birds and the water, but I was also coming here to go back *there*, to that other place. The whine of the two-stroke engine as I opened the throttle; the sheen of spilled petrol as it mixed with water in the bilge; and Dad trying to talk above the noise, telling me to go slower, or warning me about a concealed sandbank, or saying *C'mon now, we better go home.*

*   *   *

Eels are tiny when they are born, no bigger than a grain of sand, and completely transparent. If you could look through them, you would see into the world. As they grow older, though, they begin to absorb light, to bend and to capture it. Their skin darkens, their bodies lengthen, and their translucency is replaced by an oily brown. Streaks of yellow run down their flanks, like bars of muddy gold, and their eyes grow more pronounced. The grain of sand has become what is known as a 'yellow eel'.

The transformations continue, change following change. As they grow, their yellow flanks darken, shade into umber, until, reaching full maturity, they take on the colours of a starry midnight. A slick glossy black covers their top half, while their underbellies acquire a silvery sheen. Glints of brown and green cover their back like flecks of mica. The yellow eel has become a 'silver eel'.

These creatures are born in the Sargasso Sea, where they emerge from unknown depths – unknown because, despite many attempts, no one has ever seen eels mate in the wild. All we know is that they float up from sea-dark, tumbling out of tiny eggs as they rise up, and that, during these first months, they do not look like eels so much as willow leaves. (Newborn eels are known as leptocephali, meaning 'slim head'.) At first, these willow leaves are unable to swim, and so they float on the great ocean roads of the Gulf Stream and the North Atlantic Drift. These are the same currents that carried their ancestors east and that allow them to travel extraordinary distances: eels entering the coastal waters of Ireland and Britain will have travelled three thousand miles, while those that travel to Latvia, Estonia and Iceland will have gone even further, some as much as five thousand miles. Millions will perish during the two-year journey, either from predation or sheer exhaustion, but billions will also survive, and these creatures – now grown larger after many months at sea – will begin shoaling around the coasts of Europe and North Africa.

A few weeks later, the eels will migrate into estuaries, rivers and streams, while others will find their way to ponds, lakes and ditches, sometimes crawling across dry land to do so. Then they will burrow into the muddy earth, hollowing out little nests underground. These are the homes where they will stay for many years, hunting at night and resting by day.

And then, when they are sexually mature, the eels do something extraordinary. On autumn nights, when the moon is in its last quarter, and after rain has swollen the rivers, adult eels turn their noses west, abandon their dwellings, and swim for the Sargasso Sea, where they die soon after mating. It's a place they hardly know, having left it when they were only one or two weeks old, and yet it's a seascape that's written into their bodies, and to which they return with fateful precision. Beginning its life as a wayfarer, the eel ends its life as one too, and perhaps it always knew this moment would come: this strange sea-journey, this long swim home.

How might that feel, to hear the call of home from three thousand miles away? But also: what is it like for home to be in two places at once – the Sargasso Sea and a river in Europe? Like ours, the eel's heart seems to be a complex thing: wild, confused, hungry, strong.

* * *

When I first learned about the life cycle of the European Eel, I did not quite believe it. I was with some friends in a London pub, a few pints deep into a session, before my friend's partner, who had said very little that evening, began telling us about eels. The daughter of a fisherman, she had heard tall tales all her life, but told us that, as far as wild stories went, the eels' was unmatched. She then described the fish's life cycle, and we listened in the noisy pub as the eel drifted from the Sargasso Sea to Europe before swimming back again.

The story of the eels stayed with me. And somehow, over the following months, I found myself becoming steadily obsessed with these fish. I began reading about eels online and borrowing eel-books from the library, and after making my way through popular accounts on the subject, among them Richard Schweid's *Consider the Eel* and Tom Fort's *The Book of Eels*, I started wading into deeper waters, accumulating scientific articles on the animal's evolution, behaviour and life cycle.

Some of the articles were difficult to read, while a few were actually unreadable. Yet it often happened that, tucked away in an unassuming paragraph, I would come across the most incredible revelations concerning these fish. And as one article led to another, which led to yet more startling facts, I found myself talking about eels, constantly thinking about them, as well as loitering around the rivers of Bristol, where I hoped to glimpse them under a bridge or by a sluice gate. Having slipped into my consciousness, the creatures had gradually worked their way into my being, and when I finally realised what was happening, it was too late. I had become what I never thought I would be: an eel enthusiast, an eel obsessive, an eel bore.

What I found was fascinating and strange. I learned that eels have no biological sex when they arrive in Europe – something that only develops after they reach freshwater – and that there seems to be a correlation between the fish's eventual sex and its geographical location: eels that travel upstream are more likely to be female, while those that cluster near the mouths of rivers are more likely to be male. In contrast to salmon and trout, eels have also never been bred in captivity, not least because scientists have been unable to replicate the right mix of salinity, temperature and light levels to be found in their natural environments. I also learned the Sargasso Sea is bounded by a series of thermal fronts, each associated with distinctive odours, and that eels, with their powerful sense of smell, are able to discern the slightest differences between these fronts. By these means, they can distinguish the Sargasso Sea from the adjoining waters, and it is this amazing ability, supplemented by their attunement to Earth's magnetic fields, that allows them to return home with such accuracy.

There were also many curious explanations for the eel's provenance – explanations that may seem quaint to us now, but which, at the time they were proposed, were taken seriously by those engaged in the so-called 'eel question'. According to Aristotle, for instance, eels emerged through a process of spontaneous generation, rising from the fecund matter of 'mud and moist earth'. For Pliny the Elder, the process was rather different: baby eels did not abruptly appear from the earth, he claimed, but were born when flakes of skin fell to the ground after adult eels rubbed their bodies against rocks. By the time Izaak Walton published *The Compleat Angler* in 1653, answers to the eel question had spawned many new and dazzling variants. Describing a common belief, Walton writes that 'Eels are bred of a particular dew, falling in the months of *May* or *June* on the banks of some particular Ponds or Rivers', and that the dew is transformed into an eel by the power of the sun. (Other explanations of Walton's day included the idea that eels were hatched from beetles or that they were propagated when hair from a horse's tail fell into a river or stream.)

In the event, the truth was just as fantastic as the wildest theory. For what could be more unlikely than the eel's actual life – its birth as a transparent ribbon in the Sargasso Sea, its journey to Europe and North Africa across the Atlantic Ocean, its growth into an adult eel with dark flanks and a silvery belly, and then, on rainy nights, its sudden leave-taking of rivers and estuaries, so that it might die in the waters where it was born?

And yet it was not long after I started reading about these fish that I came across an astonishing fact: since 1980, the number of elvers arriving in Europe has declined by 90 per cent. Adult eels have also been struggling to return to the Sargasso Sea, thanks to the proliferation of barriers along their migratory routes, with some reports suggesting that their migrations have more than halved in abundance. Just as my research was disclosing the most fascinating things about eels, then, it was also revealing the extent to which they were disappearing from the world. The wonder and mystery deepened, but so did a growing apprehension of loss.

* * *

The Severn gleams under the moon, heavy with water, polished by light. Mist rolls from bank to bank, and in the fields beyond the river, stray cattle pass like ghosts. It is very dark and very quiet. 'They're coming,' the man next to me says. 'I can feel it.' Then he kneels down, pulls up some grass, and throws it into the river. 'In ten minutes,' he says, 'the tide will turn and the grass will float back to us. That's when we put our nets in.'

The man's name is Andy Beddoes and he's an eel fisherman. A few weeks ago, I had written to the Sustainable Eel Group, which restocks rivers with the help of local anglers. I had wanted to learn more about their work and thought they might send over some articles and reports, and so was surprised when, a week later, I received an invitation to go fishing. 'Would you like to meet some elvermen?' the chairman of the organisation, Andrew Kerr, asked me. 'They'll be going out next month and can show you things you won't find in the books.' I told Andrew I couldn't think of anything better, and after he gave my email to one of his contacts, I eventually received a brief message. 'We will be fishing the tides,' it said. 'You are welcome to come out.'

We look out over the river, hands thrust into our coats. By the banks, where the willows gather, the water is dark, but at the river's centre, where the trees do not reach, the moon hammers down its brightness. The water flows past our feet, glinting as it goes.

'Might as well gather wood for the fire,' Andy says. 'There's nothing we can do now but wait.'

We walk into the dark, scouring the banks for wood and stacking whatever we find by an old fire pit. Once we have gathered enough, Andy walks to his jeep and returns with what looks like a mini fire extinguisher.

Could it be? I wonder, squinting in the dark. *No, surely not.*

But soon I am stepping back from the pit, my face warmed by the sudden blaze. No need for kindling – Andy has brought a blowtorch to go fishing.

'Hot chocolate or tea?' he says, as if we had just entered a cafe.

'Hot chocolate,' I reply, taking a seat by the fire.

* * *

I had travelled from Bristol that morning, taking a train to Gloucester before catching a bus to Tirley, a village eight miles north. After finding my accommodation for the night – an old farmhouse that had been converted into a bed & breakfast – I went straight to sleep, though it was only 4 p.m. 'Get lots of rest,' Andy had told me. 'You're going to need it.' When I next opened my eyes, it was not to the familiar trees of my garden, birch and hawthorn, but to a paddock full of cows. House martins chattered under the eaves. The sun hung low in the sky.

I turned on the radio. The news that day – for most of the month, in fact – had been dominated by a political scandal. Across the country, British nationals had been deported from the UK or denied re-entry at its borders. Almost exclusively, those affected by the policies were people of colour, particularly members of the Windrush

Generation, and as the scandal broke, a particular quote was often discussed on the radio, an excerpt from an interview given in 2012. 'The aim is to create, here in Britain, a really hostile environment for illegal immigrants.' The words of Theresa May, the country's former home secretary and, at the time of my visit to Tirley, the prime minister of the UK.

I turned off the radio and went outside. By the farmhouse, a quiet lane took me past stone cottages and thistly fields, before turning into a small track leading into a woodland. A blackbird sang from an ash tree, and I listened as the last of the dusk slipped away from the valley. Not long after returning to the farmhouse, another text came through from Andy: 'Be ready for 10:30. And wear lots of warm clothes.'

*   *   *

It is an hour before midnight and Andy is pointing to the river. A clump of grass has drifted by, followed by another. 'There,' he says, 'the tide has turned. The elvers will start running now.' He hammers two stakes into the ground, and then plunges the net into the water. The net sits snugly on the bank, held in place by the stakes.

It doesn't take me long to realise I had been wrong about Andy. His correspondence gave the impression of a reserved and laconic man. Within minutes of meeting, though, he has already started telling me about the ways of the Severn (a river he has fished his whole life), the eels' strange habits and customs, and a dozen other topics that have come to mind: his former life as a gamekeeper on a local estate, his son's expertise at fixing computers, the state of British politics. And as we sit by the banks of the Severn, warmed by the fire, I begin to see how important this river is to him. The Severn, he tells me, is where he learned to fish with his father, where he caught his first eels as a boy, and where he has spent thousands of days and nights fishing. It is also where he went elver-fishing for the first time, on an April evening not unlike tonight.

'It had flower patterns on it,' he says, describing his first net. 'My mother was replacing her old mesh curtains, and so that's what we used. Of course, nets are very different now. Most chaps have aluminium frames and some even have theirs made of carbon fibre – imagine that! As kids, we made our frames from willow.'

I ask Andy about the Sustainable Eel Group and he describes the unlikely partnership that has formed between conservationists and traditional anglers. Whatever is caught tonight will be sold to the 'station', he tells me – a local fishery with a special licence to buy eels. Some eels will then be sold to fish farms, to be used for the restaurant trade, while the greater portion, at least 60 per cent, will be used to restock depleted rivers. Andy was thus a curious hybrid of angler-turned-conservationist, someone who was fishing for eels in order to keep them alive.

'But don't get me wrong,' he says, after I ask him a few more questions about the Sustainable Eel Group. 'I like fishing, but I'm also here for the money. A kilo of elvers can get you £150 these days, and if you have a good season on the river, well . . . you can earn back the cost of your licence and more.'

We feed more wood into the fire and stare at the flames. Later, after Andy has told me about some of the adult eels he has caught on the Severn, our conversation drifts to the topic of home. When he asks where I lived before England, I tell him about my childhood in Indonesia, and how, when I was ten, my family moved to Australia. It was a shock, I say, leaving Jakarta for the suburbs of a Queensland town. 'We went from high-rises and mile-long traffic jams to wallabies on the way to school.'

Andy nods in sympathy, as though he could relate to the experience. Before moving to Tirley, he says, he used to live along a very different stretch of the Severn, and it took him a long time before he became accustomed to his new village.

'And where did you live before moving?' I ask, expecting him to name a distant town by the Severn's upper reaches. But his answer – 'above the weir at Tewkesbury' – makes me sit up. On the train ride from Bristol, I had studied a map of the surrounding area and knew that Tewkesbury was only a few bends upriver. Andy's big migration was all of five miles.

As the night unfolds, though, I begin to appreciate how significant the move was for him, for so many of the stories he has related this evening have to do with particular stretches of the Severn, and even his description of his former home ('above the weir at Tewkesbury') has been made in relation to the river. As a boy, the river by Tewkesbury was where he first witnessed elvermen at work ('you could buy elver pie for sixpence then') and where he would go fishing with school friends, sometimes with a healthy supply of cider in their bags ('some nights we were as drunk as handcarts'). And now, as an angler in his sixties, the river by Tirley is where he continues to fish with his heavy elver nets, despite the beginnings of arthritis in his shoulders. ('You should hear me in the morning,' he says. 'I sound like a packet of crisps.') Andy was raised by the river, I realise – in more senses than one – and by the end of the night, it becomes obvious that there is more to elver-fishing than he lets on. The money may be one factor, but his connection to the Severn runs deep, reaching into his life like the long arm of the tide.

We feed more branches to the fire, watching them catch and burn down, and then, around one in the morning, Andy stands up and walks to the river.

'They're coming,' he says again, for the second or third time that night.

It's his second week of elvering and he hasn't seen a single elver all spring. But tonight is the night, he reckons; tonight the eels will come.

It is. And they do.

One hour past midnight, in a field deep in rural Gloucestershire, a net is lifted up, two faces peer down, and something precious is pulled up from the dark: an elver – frail, thin and milky-white. Andy transfers the creature into a bucket, and we pass the bucket from hand to hand.

'Go on,' he says, 'hold it.'

Before I can say anything, he tips the bucket over my hands. I watch as the elver slides down towards the rim, and then it is there, in my cupped palms. An elver – yes, an elver – three thousand miles after setting off, turning softly in my hands. I bring it up to my eyes and watch as it lifts its long, intelligent head. It is delicate and light, unimaginably tender and light, and I suddenly laugh at the sheer strangeness of it.

'Those are its eyes,' Andy says, pointing over my shoulder.

At the tip of its head I can see two dots: two pinpricks of black.

'And that?' I ask, pointing to a small mark below the eyes. There, caught in the transparency of the elver's body, is a dash of red.

'Its heart,' he says.

It floats there, wondrously clear and vital, and I fancy I can see it palpitating, expanding and contracting under the gleam of my torch.

We return the elver to its bucket and walk back to the fire. The ebb tide is moving quickly now, and along the river's centre, where the moonlight is concentrated, the water is sequined with light. The elvers are beginning to run; the season has started.

We take our seats by the fire again. Andy tells me more stories about the Severn, and at some point in the evening, we hear the cracking of a branch. Then a figure material-ises out of the dark – a ruddy face with blue eyes under a woollen hat.

He offers a brisk nod by way of greeting and sits beside us. His name is Dave, one of Andy's friends, and I learn that he has been fishing a few hundred yards away from us. Andy pours out mugs of hot chocolate, and as we wait for the drinks to cool, Dave tells us about the elvers that have come to his net – around a dozen or so. It's not a large catch, he says, given the numbers they are used to, and yet he seems excited, albeit in a gruff, understated way. Five miles downriver, Dave's son has already caught a kilo of elvers, and there are reports of similar catches elsewhere, at Maisemore, towards the mouth of the Severn, and in the River Parrett in Somerset. The first elvers have arrived, and they are hoping that hundreds – no, thousands more – will follow in their wake.

I walk down to the river, where our elver is tracing hesitant circles around the base of the bucket. Its eyes are dark and concentrated, its body graceful and lithe, and it is almost completely transparent, apart from a fine black line running through its length, which I later learn is the beginning of pigmentation. It seems very curious, fascinated by its plastic bucket. But it also seems afraid, unsure of its new world. It wants out.

I return to the fire, where the talk has drifted to the decline of fishing. The rivers are different now, Andy says, gesturing towards the banks. There are more sluice gates and dams, more concrete and more steel, and the elvers are having a harder time getting through. Dave nods while drinking his hot chocolate. There is not much we can say to that.

Later that morning, when the fishing is done, I follow Andy and Dave down to a ditch between two fields. The ditch is on the other side of a twenty-foot tidal gate, one of the many barriers separating the eels from their former wetlands. The gate, Dave tells me, is operated by remote control.

The men hand me a bucket of elvers. They have only caught twenty or so tonight, too few to sell to the fisheries, and so we have brought them here, where Andy thinks they will have a better chance of surviving. We walk to the edge of a ditch, which runs for miles into the country, and where the water is dark and cold and clear. I crouch down, tip the bucket, and watch as the elvers flutter slowly out, like flakes of snow.

* * *

Long after that trip to Tirley, images from the Severn would return unbidden – the elver's heart, the glowing embers, the moonlight on the water . . . For months, too, the world felt roomier, more alive. Suddenly a river in Gloucestershire was connected to the Atlantic, and now there was a direct line between Tirley and the Sargasso Sea.

For weeks, though, I also continued to be troubled by one aspect of my trip to Tirley. It was the news on the radio in the hours before I met Andy and Dave, what came to be known as the Windrush scandal. As more revelations came to light, it transpired that 164 British nationals – men and women who were born here, or who had come to Britain as children – had been wrongfully detained, deported or otherwise targeted by the Home Office. Long-time citizens of the country, they had woken up one morning to be told that they were not British, and that, if they could not provide the correct documents, they would have to leave their homes.

As the months passed, a strange yet persistent associ-ation formed in my mind between the declining fortunes of eels and Britain's immigration policies. These things are worlds apart – politically, historically, ontologically – and yet they seemed connected by an underlying logic: the hardening of borders and the fragmentation of home. In recent years, a group called AMBER (Adaptive Management of Barriers in European Rivers) has counted more than one million obstructions in rivers across Britain and continental Europe – obstructions that not only impede the movement of eels, but also of salmon, trout and other migratory fish. And in the last two decades, more than twelve thousand miles of fencing have been constructed along European borders, in order to keep migrants and refugees out. Increasingly, Europe's rivers are no longer apertures onto the world but barricaded waterways, while its political borders have come to resemble fortresses or citadels.

Among those affected by the Windrush scandal, it is true that some lacked documentation proving their right to remain. However, there was a simple reason for this. When their parents arrived in Britain in the 1950s, '60s and '70s, they did so under the British Nationality Act of 1948, which granted rights of settlement to anyone born in a British colony or Commonwealth state. If the children of the Windrush generation lacked official papers, it was because they had never needed them.

In 2012, though, they suddenly became exposed to the full force of the state. Two years earlier, the Conservative Party had pledged to lower net migration to 100,000 arrivals per year, and in the wake of this promise, Britain's immigration policies underwent dramatic changes. Across the country, officers were granted new and special powers, including the right to 'deport first and hear appeals later', while landlords and employees were tasked with participating in the government's monitoring programme. As these policies were rolled out, thousands of undocumented workers were caught up in the Home Office's tightening net, among them children of the Windrush generation. Unable to prove their right to remain, some were sent to the Yarl's Wood detention centre, where they were detained for months before being flown out of the country, and others, upon trying to return to the UK after going abroad, were turned back at the border. Still others were fired from their jobs, with some becoming homeless, while a number were also refused essential hospital treatment. Without any explanation, and seemingly overnight, these men and women were uprooted from the places they knew as home. 'It made me feel like I was an alien,' Michael Braithwaite told the journalist Amelia Gentleman, describing how, after living in England for more than fifty years, the government classified him as an illegal immigrant. And 'I felt like I didn't exist,' Paulette Wilson told the same journalist, after being threatened with deportation in 2015, despite migrating to England in 1968. Children when they left the Caribbean, both Wilson and Braithwaite attended school in England, worked here, raised their families in the UK, and also saw themselves as British. In the eyes of the Home Office, however, they were 'illegal aliens'. Effectively, they had become stateless in their own land.

Home: what is it, where is it? And why do some people get to decide that question for others? In the weeks after that fishing trip with Andy, I would often think of the first elver we caught that night – two years young, but already three thousand miles old; and whenever I thought of its compatriots drifting across the Atlantic Ocean, I would feel a sense of wonder at their journeys, but also a kind of world-dizziness. For eels, among the other things they do, make you reconsider geography. Crossing borders with impunity, they make a mockery of the lines we draw across the world, and though they are officially known as the 'European Eel', they are not European at all, for they can also be found in North Africa and the Middle East. And why not? After travelling three thousand miles from the Sargasso, how could they only be content with Europe, when they might as well go the extra thousand miles to the Nile or the Litani River in Lebanon? Pulling at the edges of our maps, eels stretch them into new shapes, showing us more generous ways of imagining the world.

Unwittingly, the human response to this creature of flow has been high walls and hard borders. As soon as eels begin migrating upriver, many are confronted by the riddle of dams, weirs and sluice gates – a riddle compounded by the fact that many of their wetlands have been transformed into fields. Today, elver migrations are a fraction of what they used to be, while the number of adult eels returning to the Sargasso Sea has also plummeted. As recently as the 1960s, however, elvers once visibly darkened the rivers of Europe, appearing in such numbers that, as the writer Gavin Maxwell recalls of a river in Scotland, you could dip your pail into a stream and find it filled with a 'greater volume of elvers than of water'. In Italy, too, the migrations of adult eels were so great that, according to Tom Fort, fishermen once stoked huge fires along the riverbanks, conflagrations that confused and then repelled the eels, thus giving the men more time to empty and reset their full eel-traps. Slowly, though, eels have been losing their place in our world, and as they go, they leave small but definite absences in their wake: rivers that have lost gleaming eyes, estuaries that have lost muscled tails, ponds that have been stripped of their shadows.

When I started to explore why this was happening, it became apparent that the eel's predicament could not be separated from the complex story of how Britain's wetlands have been transformed over the centuries. In part, it is a story about the successes of engineering – achievements that allowed humans to farm on the site of former marshes, and which generated extraordinary wealth for some of the people who lived there. But it is also a story about destruction and loss, since it involved the partial or complete displacement of the communities that once flourished in these places, both human and nonhuman. And as I learned about this history, I found half-rhymes between the deep past and the present, especially around the question of home – of how home is made and unmade, and the ways in which, sometimes inadvertently, sometimes knowingly, people have created hostile environments for each other and for the animals with whom they share the world.

* * *

To look at old maps of Britain is to see how much water has been chased away by centuries of human occupation.

Before the seventeenth century, the Norfolk Broads, the Lincolnshire mosses, Romney Marsh, and the fens between Cambridge and Lincoln were soft and watery places, a hinterland of pools, bogs, reed beds and peatlands. Further north, water held the Vale of York in its permanent grip, rising up from springs or accumulating as rain, while the lowlands along the Humber were periodically inundated by the high tide. In the west of England, the Somerset Levels was a '*poured* landscape', in the writer Adam Nicolson's memorable phrase, and so too were the muddy, silty lands along the River Severn. And even far inland, where seas and rivers had no say, wetness reached deep into the country – in the upland bogs of North Wales, the inland marshes of the Derwent Valley in Yorkshire, and the fenland surrounding Lough Neagh in Northern Ireland. 'About a quarter of the British Isles,' according to the ecologist Oliver Rackham, was once 'some kind of wetland.'

Centuries of human activity have profoundly altered most of these places. Across Britain, lakes and pools have been emptied, marshes and fens reclaimed, fields embanked, and a vast network of ditches scored into the land to send water back to river or sea. Formerly the largest lake in Southern England, Whittlesea Mere is now flat farmland, while the 'fenways fearful' described by the bard of *Beowulf* are farmed for beets and potatoes. Large wetlands still exist, in places such as Romney Marsh, the Doxey Marshes and the North Kent Marshes, but even these are isolated fragments of once great systems. In the last century, continental Europe has lost two-thirds of its wetlands, while the figure for Britain is an astonishing 90 per cent.

The transformations began in earnest with the Romans, who constructed the first major ditches, dykes and seawalls. To separate land from sea, they built massive embankments along saltmarshes, and to turn marshes into fields, they dug channels that hastened water into rivers and canals. In this way, they summoned fields of rye, millet and spelt out of wetland, and erected villas and farmsteads on the former habitats of otters, bitterns and eels. (In Magor, not far from where I went fishing with Andy and Dave, a Roman ship was exhumed from the mud in 1993; the ship contained cereal grains harvested sometime around 300 CE, perhaps grown from reclaimed land along the Severn Estuary.)

The reclamations continued during the Middle Ages, with thousands of drains, embankments and sluice gates appearing across the country, but it was in the seventeenth century that the most dramatic changes took place. This was when 'gentlemen adventurers' began funding large-scale projects to convert wetlands into arable land, and when engineers, among them the famous Dutchman Cornelius Vermuyden, proposed radical solutions to reclaim fens and marshes, including ten-mile-long drains that rerouted rivers away from fenland. In one landscape alone, Hatfield Chase, Vermuyden and his workers clawed back some 70,000 acres of land, and although the drainage works were often disrupted and sabotaged by distraught fenmen, who saw a whole way of life being drained before their eyes, 'progress' was unstoppable. For most outsiders, the wetlands were a wilderness – barren landscapes beyond the pale of civilisation – and it also helped that those leading the charge, the agrarian modernisers, often had the might of the Crown on their side, as well as funding from venture capitalists. The fenlanders could resist for a time, but they could not win.

The transformation of Britain's wetlands led to remarkable concentrations of power and wealth, especially for the speculators and landowners who sponsored extensive drainage projects. But the abundance came at a devastating cost for the original communities of these landscapes, who increasingly found themselves surrounded by parched land. More than anyone else, these people knew how to live with wetness – how to retreat from places seasonally reclaimed by water, and how to flourish at the edges of marshes and fens. They also knew what the outsiders could not see: that the wetlands, far from being unproductive wastes, were places of plenty. They understood that the richness of the grazing marshes was the product of winter floods, and that, though the land's laws were non-negotiable, determining how and where you could live, the wetness was also the source of life – the magician's hat out of which everything else emerged. Eel, pike and tench could be fished or trapped in the pools; wigeon, geese and snipe hunted in the marshes. Sedge, rushes and reeds could be cut for thatching, eelgrass used for cattle fodder, peat dug up and dried out for fuel, while medicine could be gathered from the land in the form of herbs. For locals, the wetlands were giving places – landscapes that collapsed softly underfoot (in East Anglia, men used to look for their cattle on stilts) as well as places swelling with the gifts of life.

The unmaking of these wetlands gradually destroyed the societies that once prospered there, from the fen people of East Anglia to the marsh dwellers of the Somerset Levels. It also meant the uprooting of the animal communities for whom these places were home. When elvers enter rivers like the Severn, many look for streams and creeks that offer access to marshes, lakes, pools and ponds. Over the centuries, however, these traditional nurseries have slowly disappeared, as wetlands have been converted into agri-cultural land. For eels, it must appear as though the world were contracting, as though the very sources of life were drying up.

Their experience is shared by many other wetland species. Formerly abundant in Britain, the crane disap-peared some 400 years ago (although it is now being reintroduced to some parts of the country); and once common birds such as curlew, lapwing and woodcock are now threatened or endangered. The country's populations of water vole, natterjack toad and otter have also declined steeply, while many native wetland plants, among them marsh helleborine, foxtail stonewort and lesser water-plantain, are fast disappearing. Today, more than a tenth of all wetland species in Britain are at risk of extinction.

Home: where is it, and what is it? And why do some people get to decide that question for others? 'Thus have strangers prevailed to destroy our inheritance,' wrote Richard Bridges in 1630, after witnessing the destruction of his village at the hands of Vermuyden, whose attempt to drain the wetlands around Hatfield led to the inundation of surrounding settlements and landscapes. And in a 1640 petition, lamenting the partial loss of the Lincolnshire fens, the locals struck a similar note: 'Our lands & inheritances are taken from us.'

These are the human testimonies of those who were displaced by the draining of the wetlands, but there are the testimonies of animals too – messages written on air, land and water, which, if we could learn to read them, would tell us about the great uprooting they too have experienced in these lands.

* * *

The golden mud and the light-struck sea. The tide surging upriver and now a flock of sandpipers above the estuary, their plumage the colour of wet ash. It is late July and I am back at Severn Beach, walking along the seawall into strong winds.

I go down to the beach and stand at the water's edge. A few miles to my left is the port of Avonmouth, all dark towers and metal cranes, and to my right, along a wide band of mud, are hundreds of birds. They are looking for worms and snails by the estuary, and from where I stand, and as the sun strikes the shoreline, it seems as though they are walking on vast iridescent sheets, a wet golden fire.

I take a photograph of the marsh on my phone, keeping the birds in the background, and try to imagine what this landscape must have been like before the Romans, long before the first ditches and seawalls. Twelve miles across the estuary, by the village of Goldcliff, archaeologists found ancient fish remains in the mud, among them eel bones that had been cooked on hot coals thousands of years ago. At the time these fish were caught, Severn Beach was a liquid empire, a vast sequence of creeks, lagoons and marshes. And it was a place ruled by the rhythms of the sea, where the river overspilled its banks at high tide and flooded miles of hinterland. They would have been huddling around a fire, those Mesolithic hunters, dozens of fish squirming in their traps as the moon rose high above them.

I put my phone away and walk on, heading north towards the old ferry terminal at Aust. Scores of dunlin race across the estuary, white bellies flashing against the sun, and beyond them are redshank, swinging far out above the water. I step on to the marsh, trying to keep my attention on the birds, but my mind has now drifted to something I heard on the radio a few months ago, and which has been bothering me for weeks. Had it not been for the eels, I might not have held on to it for so long. But because I had been thinking of these fish in recent months – their migrations, their capacity to make a home for themselves in difficult conditions – what I heard on the radio had struck me in a particular way.

It was a man talking about 'Somewheres' and 'Anywheres', terms by which he tried to explain the current state of British politics. If you are one of the 'Anywheres', he had said, then you are part of that restless tribe of the metropolitan middle class, whose identities are portable because they are not attached to certain places or communities. By contrast, 'Somewheres' are deeply rooted in tradition, community and landscape: they belong to a particular world, and it belongs to them.

In reality, the man conceded, things are more complicated – the categories are not watertight. Nevertheless, he had pressed on with his theme. The Somewheres are a place-bound people who tend to be more conservative in their politics, whereas the Anywheres, more likely to be liberally progressive, are as happy in one city as the next. And it is the tension between these two groups, he added, that partly accounts for the division and acrimony in contemporary Britain.

A flock of geese lifts up from the saltmarsh, charging the air with their wings and loud cries. They rise into the amazing light at Severn Beach, which says to you: *stop thinking and watch this show I'm putting on.* But my head is whirring, a thought-flock of words, and I can't step out of my mind, which is where I know the estuary begins. For isn't it possible to be a traveller with many miles under your belt and still know what it means to love a place – the unchanging view, the rounded horizon? And what about those who live deeply within their own bounds and remain open to the stranger? Some of the divisions between Anywheres and Somewheres are real, and some of them are also growing wider. But the terms also fail to capture the many shapes a human life might take, which are always more complex than our categories allow for.

And not only a human life. From one perspective, eels are Anywheres, wayfarers for whom the world – from the Sargasso Sea to Europe and North Africa – is a vast borderless expanse. But it would be wrong to conclude from this that eels have no deep attachment to landscape, or that they are not good citizens of place. We think of eels, if we think of them at all, as long-distance migrants, and yet many are also lovers of continuity. In 1968, scientists captured 350 yellow eels by Heligoland in the North Sea. The eels were marked, taken many miles from their home territory, and then released, and when the scientists went back a few months later they found that dozens of the eels had returned to the waters where they had been discovered. The fish is possessed of an unusual 'homing ability', wrote eel expert Friedrich-Wilhelm Tesch in 1977, discussing these and other findings. This ability, he added, is 'yet to be seen so clearly in any other species of fish' and is 'reminiscent of the qualities shown by homing pigeons'.

Home: what is it? Where is it? If I close my eyes, I can remember all the rooms of my childhood house in Indonesia. The bedroom I shared with my brother, with its chipped wooden floor and window overlooking a small garden; the morning coolness of the tiles in the hallway, so different from the hot paving stones outside; and at the entrance of the spare room, two carved Balinese doors, each panel painted a duck egg green and edged with gold paint. The same room was also guarded by a metallic turtle, its shell dented by years of knocks and scrapes, and on a table inside the room was a glass box filled with six different colours of sand, each separated by a thin glass panel. If you shook the box, the sands would rearrange themselves into new patterns, and if the sands settled in a certain way, they would take on the appearance of dunes in a desert, an effect heightened by the fact that, frosted onto the back of the glass box, you could see the outline of a turbaned man on camelback, an Oriental fantasy.

All these objects came with us when we moved to Australia: the Balinese doors, the metal turtle, the turbaned rider (although the box would shatter after a few years) as well as my mother's prayer mats, with their woven images of towering mosques and arches, their stylised depictions of trees and palms. There was also a wooden chest that my mother had bought from a Jakarta market, a darkly lacquered cabinet containing an intricate set of inner chambers (packed with her favourite jasmine tea), as well as four statues my father had collected during his trips to Kalimantan, all carved by Dayak craftsmen. As we unpacked our boxes in Australia, I remember how the smells of Jakarta were suddenly with us again, rescued from oblivion at the point of vanishing.

Those smells are still with me, in Bristol, although now they mingle with those of other countries and cultures. My partner refuses to drink any tea other than Barry's, which she grew up with in Dublin, while I have now been converted to Yorkshire Gold. And occasionally, talking late at night, we will wonder at what we are doing here, and how it is that so many years have passed for us in Bristol. 'Is this it?' we sometimes ask. 'Is this for good?' Neither of us had planned to stay in England when we left the countries where we had grown up. Both of us have now been here for more than ten years. We never thought Bristol would become home for us, but that is what has happened.

But what if you cannot go home, because home has been dismantled or even demolished? Walking along the salt-marsh, I think again of the members of the Windrush generation, whose very existence in Britain was deemed to be 'illegal', and of the men, women and children trying to cross right now from Calais to Dover, because home has become intolerable or unsafe. And I think of the perilous journeys of our animal neighbours, whose life cycles are becoming harder to complete. After leaving their ponds and rivers, hundreds of thousands of silver eels will eventually reach the Sargasso Sea, while others, finding the way blocked by dams and seawalls, will never make it back. Still others will be killed by hydropower turbines, sliced into thick wedges by the turning blades, and among these casualties will be sexually mature female eels, their bellies swollen with the presence of unfertilised eggs. Then there is the fact that the European eel is being illegally fished and trafficked in order to supply the restaurant trade in East Asia – another kind of displacement. For the creatures who meet this fate, they will have died in an alien place, far from their natural homes.

The human soul has a deep 'need for roots', according to the philosopher Simone Weil. For many, however, the experience of modernity is not rootedness, but of being stranded between home and the faraway – of longing for connection while living out the reality of homelessness. For those who are met with fear and hostility in their attempts to settle in new countries, this experience is particularly acute and can lead to a displacement that is profoundly internal as well as geographical. Despite the existence of countless obstructions, however, others manage to become rooted in the lands where they settle even as they remain connected to their old homes. These migrants become doubly placed, at home in two countries at once.

And yet – I have left the saltmarsh now and am walking towards the settlement of Aust – it is not as simple as that. In my mind, eels are ambassadors of global movement, envoys from a world without borders. But only four miles along the estuary, at the port of Avonmouth, another kind of border-crossing was taking place. Every year, this is where thousands of tonnes of jet fuel arrive from the Middle East, fuel that is sent on to Heathrow and Gatwick via underground pipes. And it is where other ships appear carrying cargo of all kinds, including coal from Australia, animal feed from Argentina as well as 'British' MGs made in China. Ecologically and culturally, there is nowhere else like the Severn Estuary. From another perspective, that of capital, it is simply a node in an international network – one of many links in a global supply chain. I had been thinking of eels as emissaries of flow, but flow can also mean economic liquidity: the ceaseless conversion of life into capital.

Maersk, Hapag-Lloyd, CMA CGM: the names of the containers on the cargo ships entering Avonmouth. The boats come from many different countries – Liberia, Russia, Gibraltar – and sometimes, after a trip to Severn Beach, I would log onto a website at home, to see which boats had visited the docks that day: the *Agia Eleni*, a bulk carrier registered under the Marshall Islands, or the *Waaldijk*, a cargo ship from the Netherlands. The economic forces propelling these ships have transfigured the planet, connecting Manila with Monaco, Paris with Phnom Penh, but as much as they have brought places together, they have partly undermined them too. Increasingly, the conditions of the 'Somewheres' living in austerity Britain – stagnant wages, rising rents, precarious employment – are also those of the migrant workers at Avonmouth docks. The so-called rootless and the rooted are both being swept up by the same global tides.

Powerful winds buffet the estuary, rippling the water and stirring the reeds. By now I have reached the old ferry terminal at Aust, where boats once transported passengers to Beachley, and in 1966, one of those travellers was Bob Dylan, on his way to Cardiff to play a show. 'How does it feel,' he would sing to his audience later that night, 'to be on your own, with no direction home?' A year after his crossing, the ferry terminal was decommissioned, made obsolete by the completion of the Severn Bridge. The pier is still there, but it is rotting into the mud now, on its way to being claimed by the estuary.

I should probably turn back at this point – the afternoon is beginning to fade and the last train home will be leaving soon. But I am seized by the urge to keep going, to walk on and on. Now Aust is behind me, and I am climbing a hill known as Potato Tump, just past the Severn Bridge. Three miles to the southwest, I can see the second bridge that was constructed over the estuary in 1996, and beyond that, just about visible, is the island of Flat Holm, first named by the Vikings more than a thousand years ago. They brought other names to this part of the British Isles, some of which are still in use – Lundy, Hasguard, Milford Haven – and although 'holm' was their word for a small island, every time I hear it, I think of 'home'.

The distant cry of oystercatchers, the tide rushing in, and now warm light running across the estuary, making the water shimmer. Earlier that day, I had received a text from my mother in Yogyakarta, which read: 'about to get ready for breaking puasa'. And maybe it was this that had got me thinking of holm and home, for today was the end of Ramadan, and 'puasa', which meant fasting, was at an end. That evening, a feast would be laid out on the tables of my mother's house, where uncles, aunts and cousins would gather to eat, a scene that would be replicated in households all over the country. 'Pulang kampung', people would have been saying to each other before the celebrations began, as they prepared to travel to their family homes. 'To return to one's home village', 'to go back home'.

Another flock edges into vision, this time a cloud of redshank. They fly in the softness of afternoon light, along-side other migrant birds who have come from Southern Europe and Africa: whimbrel, redshank, sandpiper. How do they find their way here, to these saltmarshes and this estuary? Perhaps they feel home as a rightness in the body, and perhaps that feeling of rightness is not something they can know in advance but something that has to be discovered as they move towards it. Always, for the first time, the birds have to remember what they do not know:

that *here* is body-feeling-right while *there* is something-missing, and that, once you are *here* again, the longing in your body will subside, at least for the moment. The redshank-cloud returns to earth – a hundred feet clicking into place – and then, as if in obedience to a hidden signal, dozens of oystercatchers lift themselves up and flock above the waters. I watch them fly, and as they go my body lights up with an electric pulse that is hard to name – the big pull of life's adventure.

* * *

When they describe the state of British waterways, ecologists sometimes speak of a 'lost connectivity' – the fragmentation caused to rivers by the erection of dams, weirs and other obstructions. It is a phrase that also applies to the country's wetlands. Today, only 3 per cent of the UK is covered by marshes, reed beds, ponds and other wetland habitats, although even these places are sometimes threatened by development: between 2006 and 2012, 1,000 hectares of the country's wetlands disappeared. For many wetland species, the country is a hostile environment, and is only becoming more so.

But what would a restored connectivity look like, and is it possible for wetlands and humans to flourish together? Perhaps the eels might help with this question, for they know a thing or two about flow. Their migrations depend upon the existence of open borders, while their life cycle underlines the importance of ecosystems in which uplands, rivers, estuaries and seas are all connected. 'Protecting them is a tricky business,' Emma Hutchins told me, when I visited the village of Slimbridge, fifteen miles north of Severn Beach, 'because it means thinking on much larger scales than we are used to. If we can get eels right, though, so much else will follow, because we will be joining everything together again.'

As the reserves manager at the Wildfowl and Wetlands Trust, it is Emma's job to draw up the conservation plans for Slimbridge's 650 acres of pools, mudflats and salt-marshes. And in recent years, after an ecological survey revealed a disappointingly low population of young eels, she had been turning her attention to these fish. 'The survey was an important moment,' she said, as we walked across a stretch of saltmarsh in late October. 'We know that eel numbers are declining in Europe, but we weren't sure whether the survey was reflecting this general decline, or whether Slimbridge itself was particularly difficult for the eels to access. So it made us ask: are the eels getting in OK, and are they also able to leave? And if not, what was getting in their way?'

Shortly after the survey, Emma said that she began looking at Slimbridge from an eel's perspective, imagining how the fish experienced its pools and ponds, and what kind of adjustments would make their lives easier. After evaluating Slimbridge along these lines, she and her team began making changes – lots of them. They began digging new ponds, widening ditches, and integrating some of the existing pools. They also retrofitted nearby dams with 'eel ladders', in order to connect the nature reserve with the River Severn, and installed screens on pumps, to ensure that eels were not being sucked into Slimbridge's machinery. 'We had to see this place from their perspective,' Emma said, 'which meant reconsidering lots of our assumptions.' The last thing they wanted to be was a 'sink', she added – a place so hemmed in by barriers that resident animals couldn't escape. 'That's what many of our wetlands have become, though – places cut off from the surrounding ecosystem.'

There can be no simple way of overturning centuries of ecological transformation – Emma was clear about that. The work at Slimbridge would always be difficult and slow, not least because she and her colleagues often had to negotiate with farmers, local authorities and the Internal Drainage Board – a complex mix of stakeholders who needed to be approached with sensitivity and care. It was expensive, too: a single eel ladder can cost thousands of pounds. Still, there had been signs of progress. A few months ago, some silver eels had successfully swum from Slimbridge to the Severn – something Emma could confirm because of the presence of fish sensors. And though the eels still had thousands of miles to go, they had completed a crucial part of their journey. They had found a way of leaving their habitats for the open sea, thus achieving what conservationists call 'escapement'. Pool by pool, marsh by marsh, Slimbridge was becoming a little wilder and less fragmented.

And the wetlands were spreading, Emma told me, at least in some parts of the country. In England, environmental groups were restoring former marshes in the New Forest, the Suffolk Broads and South Lincolnshire, as well as creating 1,600 acres of wetland habitat along the Essex Coast. In Wales, efforts are underway to regenerate the Anglesey and Llŷn fens, and in Scotland, conservationists have been restoring peatlands across large parts of the Flow Country. Meanwhile on the Steart Peninsula, some forty miles from Slimbridge, farmland has slowly given way to saltmarsh. In 2009, conservationists and local communities began organising a 'planned retreat' from a part of the coastline that was liable to flooding. In subsequent years, they allowed the old seawall to degrade, built a new sea defence further inland, and excavated earth and clay in order to create the environmental conditions for a future wetland. And in 2014, when the original seawall was breached at high tide, the response of the Wildfowl and Wetlands Trust was simply to let water roam over its old domain. In the months that followed, wetland plants began sprouting from the silt, and within a year more than 700 acres of wet meadow and saltmarsh had formed. In turn, the flooding provided new habitats for migratory birds and fish, and before long herons and egrets began arriving, drawn to the fish fry that appeared by the creeks. The land had become liquid once more – and, as planned, the new wetness was keeping other places dry, by creating a protective buffer between the tidal Bristol Channel and the nearby settlements of Stockland Bristol and Otterhampton. It was only one example, Emma said, but it was an inspiring one, since it showed how human communities might learn to live – and flourish – alongside wetlands once more.

In recent decades, too, a new way of thinking about rivers has emerged, one that is restoring some measure of wildness to the country's over-managed waterways. For more than a century, the prevailing belief has been that the best rivers are quick ones, since they hasten the movement of flood-waters away from the uplands. Rivers have thus been straightened, dredged and embanked, in order to increase their carrying capacity, as well as stripped of organic features that might impede the flow of water: meanders, gravel banks, multiple braids. And the interventions have worked, at least in part: heavily engineered rivers can carry much more water, and at much quicker flows, than non-engineered ones. As yearly images of a flooded Britain remind us, though, not all these developments have been successful, and in some cases they have exacerbated the very forces river managers have been trying to control. All the straight-ening and deepening has achieved one objective – getting water to move off the land as quickly as possible – but it has also displaced the problem of flooding to villages and towns in other parts of the catchment, which, although bulwarked by massive levees and embankments, are now exposed to greatly increased volumes of water.

In a country with wilder rivers, these problems would be ameliorated by the very things that have been destroyed: wide meanders, riparian vegetation and gravel beds, as well as upland ponds, marshes and bogs. And in some places, those things are now being restored. Eleven miles south of the Steart Peninsula, near the town of Williton, conservationists have been working with local landowners to slow down the flow of water across the landscape. Drawing upon the principles of 'natural flood management', they have allowed organic barriers to form in the Doniford and Monksilver, the two rivers of the valley, planted trees along the upper catchment, and helped farmers restore upstream ponds and wetlands – and their efforts are paying off. Water that once hurtled towards Williton after heavy rainfall is now being held for longer in the uplands, as well as being slowed by natural barriers in the Doniford and Monksilver. Similar projects are also underway along the River Peffery in Scotland and the Afon Merin in Wales, as well as the Severn, where 158 miles of river habitat are now being restored. In these places, water is becoming a world-making and life-enriching force again, and it is entirely possible that, with more funding and support, these projects will one day become the norm in Britain.

In one of his essays, the naturalist Richard Mabey reaches for an intriguing word when describing his admiration and respect for other animals: 'neighbourliness'. The word has 'nothing to do with anthropomorphism or manufactured empathy,' he writes, and nor is it synonymous with friendship. Instead, it is 'based on sharing a place' as well as 'the common experience of home and habitat and season.' To respect our neighbours, we do not need to understand them or indeed even like them. But if we can acknowledge that we share a world with them – and that our homelands form part of a continuum with theirs – that would make all the difference. According to Mabey, such a recognition might 'provide a bridge across that great conceptual divide between us and other species'; and perhaps it would also compel us to live more skilfully on the planet, by freeing us from what Edward Thomas called the 'parochialism of humanity'. Then we would find ourselves plunged into a marvellous realm of other beings. We would find ourselves in a world of neighbours.

*   *   *

It is night and the eels are stirring. They are gliding along rivers and streams, back towards the estuaries, feeling their way to the memory of salt. There are millions of them, cells tingling with the call of home, ready to nose out into those bigger waters, into the astonishment of the sea. This time, though, everything has changed: the rivers they leave behind, so unfamiliar at first, are the only worlds they know, whereas the Sargasso Sea, where they were born, is a place of mystery.

Low clouds over the hills; rain falling on the river; and water mixing with water, at those edgeless places where river becomes estuary becomes sea. Soon, the eels will leave this all behind. For now, though, they are waiting in the dark, eyes watching the moon.

MOTH

Many years ago, I listened to a story that left me cold with fear. It is one of the most terrifying stories I know, although it was never intended as such. It is a myth from Northern California, and I heard it late one night in Bristol, in the middle of winter.

It happened on a sleepless night. I had been sitting up in bed, listening to the radio. Parting the curtain, I remember my surprise when I saw that it was snowing, the first snowfall of the year, and then the room began to fill with odd words, spoken in a man's quiet voice:

Ravens were not they say. Herons were not they say. Woodpeckers were not they say. Then wrens were not they say. Then hummingbirds were not they say.

I turned up the radio. The snow was falling with greater intensity now, moving across the sky in great white swirls, and the voice continued with its strange list:

Then otters were not they say. Then jack rabbits, grey squirrels were not they say. Then long-eared mice were not they say. Then wind was not they say. Then snow was not they say. Then rain was not they say. Then it didn't thunder. Then trees were not when it didn't thunder they say. It didn't lighten they say. Then clouds were not they say. Fog was not they say. It didn't appear they say. Stars were not they say. It was very dark.

Waking the next morning, I found the streets covered in snow. So that really happened, I thought, stepping onto the white roads, feeling the snow compact under my weight. But the radio programme, in that bright morning air, suddenly seemed unreal. Who was the author of that tale? What story was being told? I promised myself to look it up, but for some reason I never did, and it was only years later, after I became interested in eels, and after I began to think about the question of extinction, that I remembered the story again. Then the man's voice returned, like something that had been mislaid, and I began to wonder what it had all meant.

* * *

The voice belonged to a writer called John D'Agata. He had been reading a creation myth from the Cahto people of Northwestern California and was in conversation with

Michael Silverblatt, the host of a radio show called *Bookworm*. 'It's an example of a really old trope,' D'Agata explained, 'a flood story, a creation story.' When it finishes, 'we end up in darkness', but whether 'that darkness is the beginning of the world or what happens after the world is destroyed' is never clear.

The source of the myth was a man called Bill Ray, a member of the Cahto nation. In 1906, Ray told the story to the anthropologist Pliny Earle Goddard, a specialist in the Athabaskan languages of California. Ray told other stories too: myths about Coyote and his tricks, about the making of the mountains and valleys, and about the lives of animals – diving otters, dancing elks, talking grizzly bears. The myth that had fascinated D'Agata, the story I heard during that winter evening, was called 'The Coming of the Earth'.

According to D'Agata, 'The Coming of the Earth' is a story about the power of community. The 'flood doesn't come as a punishment,' he says, 'or a warning, or even as a lesson, but instead it seems to come because floods will sometimes come – leaving us with nothing but the opportunity to rebuild. So that's what the Cahto do.' The myth imagines the fraying of the world so that, when things unravel, the Cahto will know how to mend them. This is destruction as community building, as a reminder of the human capacity to flourish again after ruin.

In a strange way, the tale also functions as a kind of creation myth, although one that works in reverse. Rather than describing life's emergence, the story narrates its disappearance, beginning with the marvels of creation – herons and woodpeckers and warblers – only to sweep them away. *Then wrens were not they say. Then hummingbirds were not they say. It was very dark.*

It is a grim list – abrupt and unrelenting. And yet all this disappearing has a weirdly paradoxical effect. By unstitching these animals from the tapestry of creation, the story calls attention to their *presence*, to the marvellous fact that they exist at all. This is life, the myth seems to say, and now this is not-life, and the more we glimpse the void at the heart of not-life, the dearer the created world becomes. Then we see more clearly the slate-blue of the heron's wing, the blackness of the raven's coat, and the woodpecker's bouncing flight. Then we remember the earth again, with its actual living beings, carrying out their lives under a changing sky. The myth affirms life by narrating its disappearance, by imagining the nothingness that might be.

After the discovery of gold in California in 1848, the Cahto way of life was violently uprooted. Territory was seized, children enslaved and entire villages massacred, sometimes at the behest of the US government. Thousands also perished from disease, while others starved to death. According to Goddard, Bill Ray's people had been 'reduced to about 150 souls' at the time of their meeting, while the Cahto's neighbouring tribes – the Wailaki to the north, the Yuki to the west and east, the Pomo to the south – fared no better. Between 1848 and 1873, 80 per cent of California's indigenous population was destroyed.

In the shadow of these events, it is difficult to read the myth in D'Agata's terms, as a tale about the power of community. For this is a story from a devastated culture, told by a man who, when Goddard met him, was in his early to mid-sixties, and who was one of the last to have heard these tales as part of an oral tradition. Increasingly, it is also difficult to read 'The Coming of the Earth' as a creation story. Estimates vary, but it is thought that thousands of species become extinct every year, with some biologists placing the figure as high as 30,000.

Stories travel and find new listeners in faraway places. As they age, they also accumulate new meanings, including some their original tellers could never have foreseen. 'The Coming of the Earth' once functioned as a strangely affirmative creation story – a myth that celebrated life by imagining its destruction. Today, it reads like a prophecy, a warning of what will happen – or what is already happening – when certain relationships are set aside or forgotten. Myth has come to resemble fact.

*   *   *

I began trapping moths in the summer of 2018, a year after I first learned about the European eel. I had joined a group of lepidopterists in west Somerset, and over the next week our hotel became a kind of field centre, where we trapped moths by night, studied them by day, and released them at dusk. In the afternoons, we walked into the neighbouring hills, from whose slopes we could see Minehead and the Bristol Channel, and in the evenings we retired to the hotel bar, where we talked about moths, read books about moths, and speculated about the moths we might find the next day. When I went to my room at night, I could see a distant glow beyond my curtains: the light of moth traps in the garden.

It was during that week that I began to understand the joys of moth-trapping and to meet those who have devoted their lives to this pursuit. The leader of our crew was one of them. In 1968, David Brown began trapping moths in Charlecote, Warwickshire, setting the traps in his parents' garden every day after school. And he never stopped. For the past half-century – through the Thatcher, Blair and Cameron years, the dissolution of the Soviet Union, and two wars in Iraq – he has continued trapping in Warwickshire, in the garden of that same house he inherited from his parents. He is, he believes, one of only two people in England who have run a moth trap in the same location for more than five decades.

The premise behind David's moth-trapping courses, which have been running since the 1990s, is simple. In the afternoons, he and his students place the traps in the garden, and the next morning they see what the night has brought. Afterwards, they go for a long walk before ending the evening at the pub. 'Beer, walking and moths,' David said of those early courses, 'the holy trinity.'

Today, most participants seem to be loyal returnees, men and women who go trapping with David every year and some of whom attended his first courses in the '90s. But interlopers are welcome too. 'Robinson or Skinner?' someone asked on my first day, wanting to know which moth trap I preferred. When I confessed that I didn't know what those terms meant – and that I had learned about the course after coming across a leaflet in Bristol – the response was sympathetic alarm on my behalf (what had I been *doing* with my life?) followed by a rush of goodwill (as if, after admitting to some terrible character fault, I had sought out and then accepted their help). And later, when they found out that I was an English teacher, a member of the group placed his hand over his heart in mock solemnity and began to recite the lines of a Keats poem: 'A thing of beauty is a joy forever.' To which someone else responded: 'Seasons of mists and mellow fruitfulness . . .'

And indeed, our days together were dreamy and mellow, languorous and slow. But it was also a week of excitement and discovery. 'Wait,' they would say, if I had blundered past an interesting tree or if a hedge required a closer look. 'There might be something here.' Then they would point out the eggs of the Hairstreak butterfly in the crook of a blackthorn stem, or uncover the caterpillars of the Fox moth under a hedge, or turn over a leaf in which moth larvae had burrowed long wobbly lines. Over drinks in the hotel bar, they also told me the most astonishing things: the capacity of moths to orient themselves in relation to the moon, their ability to detect pheromones from many miles away, and the vast journeys some species undertake during their life cycle – voyages that might take a moth from North Africa to Southern England. For the last year, I had been fascinated by the migrations of eels, but now my attention was being turned upwards, to the night flights happening high above us.

I liked being around these people, noticing the way they noticed. I liked their leisurely looking and sudden exclamations, and also their habit of leaving a sentence incomplete in order to browse a hedge. Their interest in moths verged on the obsessive and they could be extremely pedantic – one morning, a long debate ensued over whether a particular moth was a Cream Wave or a Common Wave. But they were also funny, enjoyed their beer, and shared my love of Bruce Springsteen. Above all, they knew how to walk deep into a field, and how to look for what was there. We hardly went more than four miles from our hotel at any point, and yet, during that week, the world was stretched open in new and bewildering ways.

The days passed in the same unhurried rhythm. In the afternoons, we set our traps in the garden, providing shelter for the moths by lining the boxes with egg cartons, and in the mornings, we peeled open the traps. When I looked at my first carton, I found it filled with scores of moths, some of which clung to the outer edges of the cardboard, but most of which had found shelter deep inside the hollows. The creatures were mostly brown, beige or creamy white in colouring, while others were violet, dark blue, deep orange, forest green, and they appeared in various shapes and sizes, some being large and rounded, others angled and small.

Some bore distinctive markings on their wings: bright bars of colour, swirling lines, gleaming watermarks. But many were plain in appearance and much harder to tell apart. These last moths seemed to exist on a spectrum of brownness, with very few variations in size, shape and pattern. The more we looked, though, the more certain details began to assert themselves. 'Can you see where this one gets its name?' David asked one morning, handing me a carton on which rested a grey-brown moth. I nudged the moth onto my thumb. On its wings were two bright marks, two silvery lines, but it was only after David told me to look from another angle that the marks rearranged themselves. Of course, there they were: two bright letters, two glowing pieces of script; this was the Silver Y moth. 'And what about this?' David would ask, holding another moth up to the group. 'Or this?'

And so we woke to moths, to mysteries. We would extract the creatures from the trap and then, as we passed the cartons around, David would list the assembled species – Common Quaker, Merveille du Jour, Flounced Chestnut – calling out the names as if they were the titles of visiting dignitaries. Occasionally, he would also tell us more about a particular moth, explaining how the Buff-tip fed on birch, for instance, or describing the life cycle of the Pale Tussock, remarks that could prompt long digressions about certain species he had seen in other times and places (and for which, alongside the football scores of his beloved Tottenham Hotspur, he had an unnervingly accurate memory). The roll call complete, we would place the moths back in the traps and take them indoors, where they would remain for the rest of the day, their wings so still I sometimes feared they were dead. In the evenings, though, they would convulse to life again. We would walk into the gardens, shake out the cartons in the dusky light, and watch as the change happened: hundreds of moths pouring downwards in a dark stream before peeling away into the night.

* * *

Shortly after returning to Bristol, I found a second-hand trap on eBay, a collapsible metal box that folded into a plastic briefcase. 'Not cool,' was my partner's first response, when I showed her a photograph of the trap, which the seller had captioned: 'No Time Wasters PLEASE'. Catherine's second reservation was more substantial: 'Won't it keep the neighbours up?'

But the trap was going for a song, and after talking it over with our neighbours, who promised they'd let us know if the lights kept them up, I won out in the end. It was getting late in the summer, but I knew from David that the moths would still be around, with some species flying deep into the autumn and winter. 'It makes foreign holidays impossible,' he had confided in the Quantock Hills, before explaining how, the one time he *did* leave Britain, on a February holiday to the Seychelles, he missed one of the most exciting events of recent years. 'The phone at home was jammed with messages,' he said. 'Friends were asking: Did you see it? How many did you catch? You see, there'd been a huge migration of the Levant Blackneck while I was away, one of the biggest Britain had ever seen. I'd missed it by a week.'

When it eventually arrived, our trap was smaller than I'd imagined: 50 centimetres long and 40 centimetres wide. After we started using it, though, it had the effect of amplifying the garden. Suddenly, our small backyard was connected to millions of cubic metres of sky; had become a landing strip for moths.

I spent a few nights trapping on my own, watching from the lawn chair with a mug of tea as the moths came in. Some of the species were recognisable from the Quantocks – the Silver Y, the Setaceous Hebrew Character, the Frosted Orange – but others were unfamiliar to me, and could only be identified after flicking through the colour plates of my field guide. After flying into the trap, most would crawl deep into the egg cartons, so that all I could see was the edge of a wing, although some would rest along the inner wall of the trap, their wings still, their antennae quivering.

Despite herself, Catherine became interested too. A couple of evenings a week, we would place the trap in the garden, setting it by a tree that screened us from our neighbour's house. Then, while sitting in the living room or washing up after dinner, one of us would check for recent arrivals. Often, there was nothing to see. If one or two new moths were spotted, however, some excited arm-waving would ensue, and we would both stand around the trap. Occasionally, we would also watch as more moths appeared from behind the garden wall, or, as sometimes seemed the case, floated up from the grass. They would curve towards us, frantically circle the light, and then quietly slip into the trap.

As with the Silver Y, each moth had its tell-tale signs – its distinctive gathering of light, pattern, colour. There was the Willow Beauty, with its wavering crosslines and salt and pepper wings; the Black Rustic, with its splash of white on brown-black wings; and the Box Tree Moth, whose milky white wings were edged with a brown band. Always, though, the vision of more experienced lepidopterists continued to surprise me. In their presence, more details came into view: a dash of colour by the terminal line, a tiny incision on the apex of a wing, a series of dots beneath the thorax. 'Look,' they would say. 'Can you see that mark?'

But the more time I spent with other lepidopterists, the more I realised this was a strange time to be looking at moths, for the creatures have not been doing well in Britain, particularly in the last sixty years. Last seen in Sussex in 1984, the Orange Upperwing is thought to have become extinct, while the Bordered Gothic, the Brighton Wainscot, and the Stout Dart – all formerly common moths – are likely to have vanished too. Since the 1970s, two-thirds of British moths have experienced sharp declines, while a fifth of once common species are now vulnerable or threatened. Hidden at the best of times, these creatures are now drifting into another kind of night, and later that year, when I came across a list of endangered moths in Britain, I was unexpectedly reminded of the Cahto myth:

Netted Carpet, Figure of Eight, Scarce Pug, Oak Lutestring, V-Moth.

The list continued, the beauty of the names at odds with the absences they now signified:

Pale Shining Brown, Scarce Vapourer, Lappet, Straw Belle, Dark Bordered Beauty, Sussex Emerald, Least Minor, Sub-angled Wave.

* * *

When I first moved to Bristol, I spent many afternoons in the Central Lending Library. The building was around the corner from where I lived, and whenever I needed respite from my home, a small damp apartment that faced a busy road, I would take shelter there. I liked browsing the library's shelf of recommended titles, which introduced me to W. G. Sebald's *The Emigrants* and the journals of Dorothy Wordsworth, or sitting in the small cafe on the ground floor, where I would reread the books I had brought with me from Australia – J. D. Salinger's *Franny and Zooey*, a battered copy of Jean Rhys's *Wide Sargasso Sea*.

I had my own unofficial places in the library: the corner table of the cafe, a row of desks by the library entrance, and a deep armchair overlooking Bristol Cathedral. But it was in the Reading Room, on the library's first floor, where I spent most of my time. Running along both sides of the room were columned galleries full of books, some of which stretched three storeys high and could be accessed via a metal staircase, while the chamber itself was filled with tiny nooks and alcoves, cabinets containing index cards from the library's former catalogue system, an ancient mechanical book lift, as well as a series of long tables and leather-topped desks, each equipped with its own reading light. Above, a vaulted glass ceiling spanned the length of the room, a tunnel of glass that darkened whenever clouds gathered and brightened again when they passed.

The Reading Room was grander than any library building I had seen before – a wonder-hall dedicated to books. In other ways, though, it was familiar territory. As a boy in Australia, my mother often took me to a library near our house, a small concrete building that stood across the road from a chicken shop and a video rental store. It did not have the ornate splendour of the Reading Room – the front door was slightly warped, making it difficult to pull open, while the carpet had been worn bare by years of footfall – and yet, to my fourteen- or fifteen-year-old self, it was a kind of palace. I would go there once or twice a week, roam the shelves on my own, gather all the books that appealed to me, and then take home as many titles as our library account would allow. I don't think the books I chose were ever to my mother's taste – at that time, I was obsessed with comics and fantasy novels – but she encouraged my enthusiasm anyway. All that mattered to her was that I liked these books, although, looking back now, I see that these books did other things for me – that they fed my curiosity, made time move in different ways, and opened up portals to other worlds. In all those years, I can't remember my mother ever encouraging me to read more 'serious' or 'literary' books, and I continue to love her for that.

After that moth-filled week in the Quantock Hills, I resumed my old habit of regular visits to the Reading Room. I was intrigued by the names of moths I had learned from David – Frosted Orange, Powdered Quaker, Dingy Footman – and wanted to learn about their origins. (I later learned that the names were not invented by Victorian entomologists, as I had assumed, but by seventeenth- and eighteenth-century naturalists who, working at a time before the Linnaean system of taxonomy had taken hold, were able to endow moths with solidly English names.) At the same time, I also wanted to know why the species David once caught in abundance as a young man were disappearing from Britain, and how other moth species were faring. Invariably, though, one title would lead to another, which led to yet others, and before long my desk was filled with dozens of books, including studies on the invention of street lighting in the nineteenth century, the development of synthetic pesticides in the twentieth century, and various changes in British agricultural practices over the last two hundred years. And as my research continued to expand, in what seemed like an endlessly ramifying series of circles, with one realm of inquiry opening to many others, I began to see that the story of moths in Britain could not be separated from the story of modernity, and that their lives, as much as ours, have been profoundly altered by transformations in agriculture and land use, developments in science and technology, and much more general changes in our relationship with nature. The teetering pile of library books was proof of the old environmentalist cliché that everything is connected, which, in the gathering darkness of the Reading Room, no longer felt like a platitude but an intricate and surprising truth.

The term *Lepidoptera* comprises two Greek words: 'lepis', scale, and 'pteron', wing. It was coined by the Swedish naturalist Carl Linnaeus in 1735 and was used to describe one of the most distinctive features of butterflies and moths: the overlapping scales that cover their wings. A single wing may contain more than a million scales, with the average scale measuring some 100 x 50 micrometres, and the complex structure of these scales also accounts for another distinctive feature of Lepidoptera. When light falls against their wings, it scatters against the scales' microscopic ridges, and the effect of this diffraction is to emphasise certain wavelengths of light while cancelling out others. The iridescence of a wing is not the effect of pigments, then, but of light scattering against the intricacy of form.

The word 'scale' has many connotations in English. It can refer to the tiny plates that cover fish, reptiles and Lepidoptera; it can refer to an apparatus for weighing or balancing; and, in another usage, it can describe gradations within a series, as when we talk about a musical scale. In this latter sense, scale is derived from the Latin 'scala', meaning to climb or ascend a ladder, and the more I learned about moths, the more this meaning of scale came to fascinate me. The reason we know that a moth's wing contains up to a million scales is because of the invention of the microscope, which allowed us to climb down into new orders of existence, and the reason we know that moths are struggling in Britain is because of long-term studies that have monitored the fortunes of different populations over decades. And there is a sense in which, to understand the complexity of our ecosystems, we have to become skilled in the art of moving between different scales of reality, so that we can begin tracing the connections between the microscopic and the macrocosmic. The moths that come to your garden contain miniature worlds on their wings: elaborate lines, extravagant patterns, delicate colours. But their presence also tells a story about the health or otherwise of the surrounding landscapes, and if we could follow the subtle chains of cause and effect that join the smallest things to the largest things, as well as all the infinitesimal inter-mediary stages in between, we would see the many ways in which our lives affect the lives of moths. Perhaps we would also see the impossibility of separating 'there' from 'here', or 'them' from 'us', for we would understand that everything really is connected, like an endless series of overlapping tiles.

* * *

It is already dusk by the time I reach the woods. I find my friends at the end of a small road, where we have agreed to meet, and after exchanging our hellos we unlatch a wooden gate and step into the woodland. It is a warm autumn evening, a few months after that week in the Quantock Hills, and the clearing we are looking for is two miles away, at the end of a long narrow track.

At first, we walk side by side, talking as we go along. Later, the path forces us into single file, and the conversation trails off. Trees float towards us in the dusk light, sudden trunks that rise upwards and thin out into branches, and above the canopy we can see a sliver of moon, emanating a cold blue light. We walk deeper into the woods, as though putting out to sea.

Gradually we turn on our headlamps. Now four beams radiate from the path, sweeping across the gloom, and for a moment, after watching my light slip off a tree into the space beyond, the thought occurs that some of the trees are moving, only stopping when our lights touch them. We keep going, hardly speaking now, and after a mile or so, when I look back at the path, I find that it has dwindled into a strip of unreality, a thin rope slung across the darkness. I stand there for a moment, turning my light on and off, so that the path vanishes and reappears again. Then my companions call out my name, 'Michael, why have you stopped?', and the world hardens into being again.

After another mile we finally come to a large clearing. We unpack our things – sandwiches, a bedsheet, a portable light – and set to work. First, we string up the sheet, using twine to fasten it between two trees. Then we place the lamp beneath it, angle the bulb upwards, and turn on the light. It burns weakly at first, a faint yellow pulse, but within minutes it has worked itself into a brilliant flare, too vivid to look at. We return to our rucksacks and sit in a circle, sharing cans of beer. Twenty feet away, a white sheet hovers between two trees, a ghost sail in the woods.

I glance at the trees beside us. While we were setting up our trap, the clearing had felt spacious to me, but now that we are idle again, it seems to have shrunk, as though the tree-line has moved towards us. We begin to talk, thinning the silence with our voices, and then, as if some kind of complication had entered the woods, the space around the clearing begins to change. The night stretches and bends.

The moths come in twos and threes, and from all directions; and they come like dreams, like visions, like snow. Some fly in frenzied circles around the light, while others move towards the bedsheet in a curving line; and as scores of moths begin to land, more continue to appear at the edges of the woods. We watch as they come, their eyes shining in the dark, and although some emerge only to vanish again, many more are drawn towards the light. These fly with a strange determination, their whole beings thrown into the effort, and yet, as soon as they land on the sheet, they become immediately subdued, as if some great thirst in them has been quenched.

A voice speaks, announcing the names of the moths on the sheet – a Dark Arches, a Heart and Dart, a Common Wave – and the spell of the night is broken. Discussions ensue, identification keys are consulted, and we begin to speculate about another moth: Copper Underwing or Svensson's Copper Upperwing? I pick up my book and leaf through the colour plates. No good: the illustrations of the two moths seem identical.

We glance at the most experienced lepidopterist of our group, who walks up to the sheet, cajoles the moth onto his finger, and considers it with a frown. 'Svensson's,' he says, with a note of finality. 'The palps are slightly darker.'

98

The matter settled, we take more cans of Red Stripe from our rucksacks and sit with our backs to the light. Then we begin to talk about the football match we are missing, the Liverpool vs Everton derby, although it is not long before our conversation drifts to other topics: austerity, the problems of the Labour Party, Brexit. As we sit there more moths enter our island of light, to join their neighbours on the sheet.

The night passes, our chatter mingling with the mysteriousness of the moths' arrivals; and at one point, after walking into the woods to relieve my bladder, I catch a glimpse of the stars, which, rather than being static, seem to be spinning towards the edge of the sky. And as the stars swirl, and as more moths float into the clearing, it is as though the woods have come alive, as if everything were alive and moving and part of a swirling whole. The moment passes, the sky becomes still again, but for the rest of that evening a residue of that world-drunkenness remains, that sense of things being multiple and strange and more than we knew. In the clearing, the bedsheet continues to ripple in the wind, a rectangle of suspended light.

We drink more beer, occasionally inspecting the sheet to see what new moths have arrived. Then, towards the end of the evening, a sudden surge of moths materialises, so many that we cannot count them. They appear like the outriders of some great detonation, a silent explosion in the woods, and as we stand by the sheet, it is as though we have walked into the centre of a storm. The moths continue surging towards the light, a summer blizzard in the clearing, and then, just as quickly as they had appeared, the flurries subside and the creatures enter as they did before, in intermittent waves of ones and twos.

We put away our field guides and finish our last cans. Then we shake the moths from the sheet, turn off the lamp and retrace our steps through the woods. We part ways after reaching the main road and, later that night, as I lie in bed, my mind is filled with the powdery wings of moths. Thousands upon thousands of them, riding the night-winds beneath the stars.

* * *

A few months after that night, I travelled to Harpenden, twelve miles north of London. I was with the entomologist Chris Shortall and we were looking at a large glass case mounted on four wooden posts. 'Have you heard of Rothamsted?' David had asked a few weeks earlier, when I called him on the phone. We were discussing the fortunes of Britain's moths, and when I asked when the first declines began to occur, he told me about a research institute in southern Hertfordshire. 'If you really want to know,' he said, 'that's where you should go.'

The structure that Chris and I were looking at was a moth trap, the first of its kind to be established here. It was designed by British entomologist C. B. Williams, who first deployed the trap in the 1920s, during fieldwork in

Egypt. In the 1930s, Williams took up a post at Rothamsted, and it was here that, after adapting and perfecting his design, he began luring the moths of Hertfordshire into his brilliantly lit glass cases.

At first, there were only three traps at Rothamsted, but after Williams retired in the 1960s, two of his successors, C. G. Johnson and L. R. Taylor, continued and expanded his work. They secured funding to buy more traps, trained volunteers to help with the monitoring, and then began transforming the project into a truly national network, by establishing stations across England, Northern Ireland, Scotland and Wales. There are now seventy-four traps on the go, Chris explained, all of which have been running non-stop since 1968.

Alongside the Light-Trap Network, Chris also oversees the operation of aphid suction traps. 'They're basically huge vacuum cleaners,' he said, pointing to a metal tower in another field. 'They pull down all the aphids flying overhead and deposit them at the base of the tower.'

The suction traps were another legacy from Johnson and Taylor, both of whom were inspired by the 1962 publication of *Silent Spring*, Rachel Carson's damning account of how pesticides were poisoning North American farms and landscapes. In the US, the book roused unprecedented levels of public concern, motivated thousands to join grassroots networks and activist organisations, and also led to the nationwide banning of DDT. For Johnson and Taylor, it precipitated a much quieter form of activism: the use of data to protect Britain's wildlife. If farmers could be alerted when aphids were and weren't on the wing, they reasoned, then those farmers could be induced to apply pesticides in a much more limited and targeted way. And if they could generate a vast archive of the country's moth populations, they would be able to demonstrate, with unprecedented detail, the effects of human activity on their populations over time. A study at the scale Johnson and Taylor were proposing, however, had never been attempted before, and the challenge facing them was immense. Ahead lay many years of sampling and counting, sampling and counting.

The slow, methodical and laborious work continues today. Each morning, Chris and his team count all the moths and aphids that have been captured by Rothamsted's traps and suction towers. They then tally up the results, feed the numbers into a vast database and share their data with farmers, scientists and environmental organisations. Afterwards, the creatures are placed in jars of ethanol and sent to the basement to join generations of other insects, some of which were flying in the skies in the 1960s.

As the institute's chief entomologist, Chris has a unique view of the United Kingdom: he can travel back in time, using Rothamsted's data as a kind of portal into the past. 'We have records for what happened every day since the late 1960s,' he said. 'And not only how many moths were trapped at particular sites, but the number of individual species. We know what happened on a particular night in

Aberystwyth, for example, or what happened on the same night on the Isle of Arran.' He told me that, since the 1960s, the network has involved hundreds of entomologists, trapped millions of moths over four million nights of recording, and recorded more than 1,500 different species.

When I asked where the traps were based, Chris recited a long list of place names, extending from Cornwall to Perthshire. I wrote down some of the names in my note-book – Wisley, Aberystwyth, Glencoe, Guernsey – but there were too many to list, and as Chris named more sites – Yarner Wood, Westonbirt, Kielder – a new version of the country lit up in my mind, an archipelago strung together by moth traps.

To my surprise, I learned that most of the network is run by volunteers. Each morning, amateur naturalists check their assigned trap, record the total number of moths and individual species, and send their results to Chris and his colleagues. 'There are a few people we pay for their time,' Chris said, 'professional entomologists who help with the identification and counting.' For the most part, though, the project is run out of sheer devotion, by people who like being around moths. One volunteer, Chris told me, has been part of the network for forty-six years.

I glanced up at our surroundings. Beside us the hedge was rustling with sparrows, and beyond the hedge were more fields, a patchwork of green and yellow that stretched towards the horizon. An ordinary English landscape, on an ordinary day. And yet the impression of ordinariness was misleading, for the data collected by the Rothamsted Light-Trap Network contains catastrophic news. It shows that the total abundance of moths has decreased by 28 per cent between 1968 and 2007; and it also shows that nearly 40 per cent of the country's species have lost half of their populations, with the declines especially pronounced in the south of England. An awful thinning has long been underway – and the losses are only getting worse.

When I asked Chris to explain the declines, he told me that they were the consequence of many of things happening at once, all of them intersecting in complex ways. In the last sixty years, the habitats that moth species depend upon – particularly wetlands, grasslands, meadows, woodlands and low-lying heaths – have become increasingly fragmented, either lost to urbanisation or converted into agricultural land. At the same time, we have become increasingly reliant on pesticides and artificial fertilisers, chemicals that accumulate in the soil and gradually permeate the foodplants of moths and other insects. Light pollution may also be a factor, Chris added, since it may be interfering with the capacity of moths to disperse and mate. And on top of all this, there was the question of climate change, which was gradually changing the distribution of species across the country.

'There have been some winners,' Chris said. 'Some species such as the Jersey Tiger and Oak Processionary are thriving with the warmer weather, since it allows them to expand their range.' He also told me that the Footman moths have benefited from successive Clean Air Acts, especially the Dingy Footman and Buff Footman, while the populations of certain species, including the Spruce Carpet and Least Carpet, have increased significantly. In the main, however, it has been a story of disappearance and loss. The records indicate that more than half of Britain's species are in decline, with some species losing as much as 98 or 99 per cent of their populations.

When I saw my first moth trap in Somerset, I hadn't expected to find so many creatures – on one occasion, we counted forty-five moths on a single egg box. After meeting Chris, though, I began to realise that my idea of abundance was an impoverished one. Looking at the Light-Trap data, it became clear that the best records were from many years ago, when the night skies were very different. During a summer night in 1976, a recorder in Yarner Wood, Devon, counted 4,681 moths in one trap – an astonishing number. Two years later, the same recorder found 103 species in the same trap, a record that far outstripped the fifty species David and I counted in the Quantock Hills. I also learned that, during a year of trapping in 1988, a trap in Warehorne, Kent, attracted no fewer than 450 moth species. The numbers were hard to fathom – what was it like to be a recorder at Warehorne or Yarner Wood during these years? – and also made me rethink my own notions of abundance. The storm of moths I had seen in the woods near Bristol, or during various expeditions with David, was in fact a much-diminished force.

From the 1990s onwards, the Rothamsted data reveals a clear pattern: a levelling off and then a decline in the abundance of Britain's moth populations. Occasionally, there are bumper nights – nights that almost rival the records from the 1970s and '80s. But such evenings have become more infrequent over the years, while the diversity of moth species being found (as distinct from total moth abundance) has steadily declined. To this day, the 1978 record from Yarner Wood – the discovery of 103 species in one trap – has never been equalled, and nor has the institute been able to improve on 1976, the year when the greatest number of individual moths (629,869, to be precise) was trapped. What instruments we have agree: from north to south, and east to west, many moth species are retreating from Britain.

* * *

There is something melancholy about encountering a moth late in the evening. The light of the world is gone; one is alone in one's room; and a tiny being is fluttering at the window, drawn to the light of the lamp. On such summer nights, it is possible to feel immense pity for something one does not really understand, to feel moved by the littleness of life. But the pity is compounded by a slight fearfulness, which is the awe one feels before the vast agencies acting upon the moth and propelling it through the world. Surely the world is too big for moths, one thinks; surely there must be more shelter, more respite, for beings such as this. So one opens the window and lets the creature in. Watches as it swims around the lamp, before finally settling on the lampshade. There is now twice as much life in the room as there was before.

If moths could speak (and they can and they do) they would tell us the most marvellous things: of night flights over mountains and valleys, of the steadiness of the moon by which they navigate the sky, and of the pheromone trails that light up the world like lanterns suspended in air. But they would speak of other things, too: the confusing brightness of our lights; the pesticides leaching into the ground and spreading through their bodies; the slow disappearance of their own kind. And if our senses were finer, and our imaginations more acute, perhaps we would feel what moths feel as they fly above a woodland or a field: a wrongness in the air, a feeling of life being undermined at one of its sources. The Black V Moth, the Union Rustic, the Scarce Dagger – for these moths, life in Britain has literally become impossible. And now many of their fellows – the Black-veined Moth, the Reddish Buff, the Speckled Footman – may be following them into the night.

In his poem 'An August Midnight', Thomas Hardy recounts a meeting with a group of insects: a longlegs, a dumbledore, a fly and a moth. Observing them as they crowd around his desk – 'in this still place / At this point of time' – he is quietly surprised by a thought, one that seems to arrive with the unexpectedness of one of his midnight guests. Insects are not the primitive or mindless things they are often made out to be, but creatures who are deeply immersed in mysteries and experiences we will never fathom:

'God's humblest, they!' I muse. Yet why?
They know Earth-secrets that know not I.

The poem ends on that note of mystery and awe, and with a startled sense that our usual ways of thinking about insects are profoundly inadequate. We are surrounded by 'small kingdoms', Mary Oliver wrote some eighty years later, describing her experience of seeing a moth in a woodland, and her contemporary, the Swedish poet Tomas Tranströmer, had a similar apprehension. 'I learned that the ground was alive,' he says of his boyhood infatuation with insects. 'I moved in the great mystery.'

From time to time, we glimpse the edge of the outline of one of these secrets, and what we learn is truly miraculous. In recent years, studies have shown that the wings of certain moths have evolved to absorb the echolocations of bats, a development that effectively cloaks them from their predators. Recently, entomologists have also found that the Silver Y moth is able to discern the direction of the winds, and that they reliably take to the air when the wind is blowing southwards in the autumn. These winds help them migrate to Southern Europe or North Africa, and in the coming spring, their descendants will return to Europe on northbound winds, resuming a cyclical migration that has taken place over millennia. It is a remarkable thought: when silver eels are returning to the Sargasso Sea, the Silver Ys are sailing the winds hundreds of feet above them.

Then there is the moth's extraordinary capacity to detect pheromones from great distances – something vividly demonstrated for me in rural Shropshire. I had joined David and some students on another mothing trip, and we were standing in the garden. 'Just wait a few minutes,' David said, heading off to his car. When he reappeared, he held a paintbrush in one hand and a can of Lyle's Black Treacle in the other, and as we followed him from tree to tree, he painted thick strips of treacle onto several tree trunks. Afterwards, we retired to the pub – 'beer being an essential part of the process', according to David, and an hour later, when we returned to the garden, we found the trees bristling with dozens of moths, sipping at the gleaming treacle with their long proboscises. Somehow, they had been alerted to chemical effusions of sugar in the air, and although I had trouble telling the moths apart (at least six different species were present, David said), it was wonderful to see them there, summoned into presence from nearby fields. And later that night, when I inspected the trees after the others had gone to bed, the moths had been joined by other insects, including a pair of earwigs, a daddy long-legs and a large black slug, the last of which left a treacly slime-trail of its own. For some time I watched them with the light of my phone, a voyeur at their midnight feast.

How had these insects come to the trees? And what distances had they travelled? In the early twentieth century, when entomologists began to investigate the enigmas of insect communication, they began to discover the most astonishing processes at work. They learned that by 'dancing' in a particular way in relation to the sun, foraging honeybees were able to communicate the precise sources of nectar and pollen to their fellow bees; that ants 'spoke' to each other via pheromone signals, by which means they could alert each other to the presence of danger or the location of food; and that the antennae of male mosquitoes were able to detect the wing vibrations of female mosquitoes flying nearby. And the more scientists looked, the more wonders opened up before them. In the late 1920s, when entomologists began taking to the skies in aeroplanes, they found insects at the most incredible heights, including moths at 3,000 feet, aphids at 5,000 feet, and wasps at 10,000 feet. 'All of a sudden,' the writer Hugh Raffles says of these findings, 'the heavens had opened.'

It was by accident, though, that one of the most important entomological breakthroughs occurred. It happened one summer evening in 1916, when Europe was at war, and when the French entomologist Jean-Henri Fabre was called into the next room by his son. '"Come quick!", the boy scream[ed],' as Fabre recalled in his book

Souvenirs Entomologiques. '"Come and see these Moths, big as birds! The room is full of them!"' Entering the room with a candle in hand, Fabre witnessed the most remarkable scene:

> With a soft flick-flack the great Moths fly around the bell-jar, alight, set off again, come back, fly up to the ceiling and down. They rush at the candle, putting it out with a stroke of their wings; they descend on our shoulders, clinging to our clothes, grazing our faces. The scene suggests a wizard's cave, with its whirl of Bats. Little Paul holds my hand tighter than usual, to keep up his courage.

It did not take Fabre long to understand what had happened. Earlier that day, he had watched a moth emerge from a cocoon in his study – a female Great Peacock moth. When he left his study that evening, however, he forgot to close the window, and somehow, although it would take Fabre years to explain exactly how, the male moths in the surrounding fields knew a potential mate was close by. And so they came, despite stormy weather, and despite the obstacles between them and the house, among them a row of plane trees, a lane 'thickly bordered with lilac and rose trees', and 'clumps of pine and screens of cypresses'. 'It is through this tangle of branches,' Fabre notes, 'in complete darkness, that the Great Peacock has to tack about to reach the object of his pilgrimage.'

The transformation of Fabre's study into a 'wizard's cave' raised many questions that would come to preoccupy the entomologist. Had the moths found their way by sight, he wondered, because they could perceive 'certain rays unknown to common retinae'? Or were they able to hear 'delicate vibrations' and 'passionate quivers' in the air, sounds that, with the aid of 'an extremely sensitive microphone', humans might also potentially hear? Or perhaps the moths were equipped with a kind of wireless telegraphy (a recent invention in Fabre's day) and could communicate via electric or magnetic signals? After four years of experiments, in which he considered these and other possibilities, Fabre finally concluded that the mechanism must be smell. The female moth was emitting chemical signals in the air, he hypothesised, and it was these signals that the male moths were picking up from many miles away. The sky for them was a medium of messages, a flexing field of meanings and signs.

In essence, Fabre was postulating the existence of what we now call pheromones. It would take five more decades, however, before scientists were able to isolate the compounds by which moths communicate with each other, and many additional studies until they could identify the different pheromones that moths produce, from chemical signals known as 'recognition pheromones', which indicate a moth's species and sex, to 'trail pheromones', which help certain moths map out routes in the sky. But how and why did moths evolve these abilities? And how is it that some can discern the direction of the winds, while others can evade the discriminating echolocations of bats? In truth, our knowledge of moths remains fairly primitive, even with all the technology at our disposal. We know many things about them, but there are countless 'Earth-secrets' we do not know, enigmas our investigations have yet to unravel and perhaps never will.

And yet, if many of these mysteries will always be beyond us, there are also secrets that we are aware of and that, from time to time, we may even experience for ourselves. 'I know nothing, nothing in the world, equal to the wonder of nightfall in the air,' Antoine de Saint-Exupéry writes in *Wind, Sand and Stars*, a book based on his experience of flying across the Sahara and the Andes as a young pilot. At such moments the 'earth rises and seems to spread like a mist' and the 'first stars tremble as if shimmering in green water'. Later, the glimmer of stars 'hardens into the frozen glitter of diamonds', and later still the sky will be filled with the 'soundless frolic of the shooting stars'. 'In the profound darkness of certain nights,' Saint-Exupéry continues, 'I have seen the sky streaked with so many trailing sparks that it seemed to me a great gale must be blowing through the outer heavens.'

* * *

It is early November and I am in the Reading Room again. On the desk are sheaves of paper containing my scribbled notes and a stack of library books, including titles on the history of entomology, the transformation of the British landscape after the Second World War, and the loss of dark skies over Europe. My curiosity about moths had led me into the fields, first to David's course in Somerset and then to Chris's research institute in Harpenden; and then, by degrees, the moths led me back to the library, since it was impossible to understand the declines in their populations without making sense of other transformations in this country, from the intensification of agriculture from the 1940s onwards (during which Britain lost more than 95 per cent of its wildflower meadows and around half of its hedgerows), to the effects of pesticide use, urbanisation and light pollution. I started off with moths, but ended up with a larger history of Britain.

I think back to that first week of trapping in the Quantock Hills, the strangeness of hundreds of moths clinging to their egg boxes. And I try to remember those afternoons in the hotel dining room when we studied the markings of their wings with our magnifying glasses. At times, during those hours of concentration, it seemed as though we had entered a library together, with each of us voyaging into the distinctive landscapes of the moths' wings, poring over the letters of a new and strange alphabet. There were the strict geometric lines of the Feathered Gothic, which seemed to have been drawn with a ruler, the fine dark specks along the edge of the Riband Wave, and the bright central plates of the Frosted Orange, illuminated panels which glowed with the sheen of tarnished gold. Beauty stretched across the surface of things, hiding in plain sight.

I had taken photographs of my favourite moths, using a magnifying glass as a kind of zoom lens. And later, when I uploaded the images onto my computer, I was able to amplify the wings on my screen and perceive new levels of detail. Certain creatures were veined with thin delicate lines, their complex branching structures like the veins of the leaves they lived upon, while others were covered with tiny dots and dashes, some of which gleamed like grains of quartz. Then there were patterns that resembled the batik sarongs my grandmother used to wear in Indonesia – branching black and brown lines against a yellow background – and, at the right magnification, the bolt of blue on the Clifden Nonpareil looked exactly like one of Rothko's field colour paintings. Some wings were also covered with the thick swirls of marbled rock, while other wings were rippled with the same wavy patterns that the wind makes against the sand, and the details were all so unlikely, so outrageous, that they seemed like things glimpsed in a dream. By zooming in, I could step down into another world, and on a few occasions, after an evening spent looking at moths this way, I would go to sleep with their wings before my eyes. Whenever I tried to concentrate on a particular moth, though, it would morph into a different being, which would transform into another, so that the Brimstone gave way to the Common Carpet, which gave way to the Powdered

Quaker ... Moths beyond moths, fluttering gently in the subconscious, their wings pressed against my brain.

In one of his poems, Samuel Taylor Coleridge describes the world as 'one mighty alphabet', a realm saturated with meaning and implication. For Coleridge, reality is a spiralling metaphysical poem, where all matter resonates with spirit, and where, since the universe is imbued with a kind of divine grammar, 'all that meets the bodily sense' is 'Symbolical'. As it is, most of these symbols escape our attention. This is because we find ourselves in a 'low world', according to the poem, 'placed with our backs to bright Reality'. We may be surrounded by the letters of the mighty alphabet, then, but since we were equipped with 'infant minds', we cannot always perceive them. Our task, for Coleridge, is to learn to see the world again with 'young unwounded ken'.

When I chanced across Coleridge's poem, it helped me understand what might be at stake in the disappearance of moths. For one of the poem's implications is that the world has a kind of grammatical structure, aspects of which can be seen and read, but other parts of which remain illegible to us, not because they are incoherent, but because they are inaccessible to our minds. And although the connection is admittedly idiosyncratic, what Coleridge's poem offered was a framework for thinking about the 'letters' on the wings of the Silver Y or the L-album Wainscot, as well as the markings on other moths, not all of which we could see or decipher. Might not all these letters and marks be part of the world's 'mighty alphabet', symbols which contribute to reality's depth and meaning? As more moth species continue to decline, however, that reality is correspondingly diminished. Letters of the alphabet begin to peel away, prised from their former places in the helix of life, while vital words are lost from its lexis.

Of course, secular readers no longer see the world in Coleridge's terms, as a realm filled with divine meanings. The universe is not a text. Nevertheless, some of us may still feel the intuitive force of this idea, even in a scientific age. Instead of 'mighty alphabet', read 'genetic codes', and in place of 'symbols', read 'biosemiotics', the study of the various means – cellular, chemical, electrical, acoustic – by which organisms communicate with each other and interpret the world. Not the thinning of a divine alphabet, then, but the unravelling of another kind of grammar: evolution's intricate and variegated productions, developed over unimaginable aeons of time, writ large and small in the forms, colours and shapes of our animal neighbours. This is the mighty world we are losing now, in all its richness and complexity.

I look up from my desk in the library. It is getting late now, the Reading Room is filling with a dusky light, and soon it will be time to leave. But as I sit there thinking about Coleridge and alphabets and moths, something else comes to mind. Earlier that afternoon, I had gone to the ground-floor cafe and come across a sign on the stairwell:

'Save our libraries'. I had passed the sign many times before, but hadn't taken it in until today, and when I stopped to read it, I learned of the hundreds of libraries that had been closed during the government's prolonged campaign of austerity. The sign went on to list a series of events during which writers, artists and storytellers would discuss the influence that books had on their lives.

I look at the small tower of books on my desk. Since my trip to the Quantock Hills, I had been reading about moths, trapping them in my garden, and learning about the causes of their disappearance. But another kind of vanishing was also taking place: the loss of those institutions that give shape and meaning to public life. These two kinds of disappearance are vastly different, yet they are also linked, since both are enabled or indeed accelerated by austerity, from funding cuts to institutions such as the Environment Agency and Natural England, to the loss of funding for libraries. Both also involve an enclosure of the commons – the disappearance of the meadows, heaths, woodlands and grasslands in the case of moths, and, in the case of humans, the loss of the public spaces that constitute and enrich our cultural ways of life. What happens as these commons go? What worlds do they take with them?

Between 2010 and 2019, 773 libraries were closed in Britain. The closures happened across the country – Cornwall, Durham, Lancashire, Northumberland, Carmarthenshire, Aberdeenshire – and devastated the many communities that had come to depend upon these institutions. Ultimately, not all these closures were successful. Thanks to volunteering efforts from local residents, some libraries that were closed eventually opened again, while others were transformed into cafes and community centres. In places where the closures were permanent, though, cities and towns lost a vital part of their imaginative hinterlands. The communal silences of reading rooms disappeared, and the books that librarians once stacked on the shelves, those small portals into other worlds, were either pulped or sold off. Since the Conservative Party came into power in 2010, there are 14 million fewer books in England's public libraries.

In the event, Bristol escaped the worst of the library cuts. Only one cherished institution, a mobile library that had served the neighbourhoods of Barton Hill and St George for more than fifty years, was decommissioned. For a moment, though, the damage could have been much greater. In 2017, the council announced that seventeen of the city's twenty-seven libraries were facing possible closure, but this calamity was averted when, in the face of a campaign mounted by the city's residents, the council was forced to reconsider its plans. In other towns and cities, however, local authorities found themselves with little choice: either they had to close libraries or divert funding from other essential services such as emergency housing and social care for children. Across the country, it was as though local authorities were faced with one of those philosophical conundrums in which one is asked to choose between two equally unacceptable outcomes, except that, since there was nothing academic about these decisions, the closures affected communities in multiple and long-lasting ways, many of which are hard to measure and which are still with us today. According to Polly Toynbee and David Walker, the years between 2010 and 2020 constitute nothing less than a 'lost decade'.

The Bordered Gothic, the Brighton Wainscot, the Orange Upperwing: these are some of the moths that have disappeared from Britain in the last century. But there are social extinctions, too – the loss of human forms of life that sustain particular ways of doing and making and being. The list of endangered moth species in Britain is long and getting longer, but as I sat in the Reading Room that evening, I found myself looking at another kind of list, composed of libraries that have closed in recent years. It is a dismal catalogue – all those dismantled bookshelves, all those vanished rooms – and, to my mind, it bore a strange resemblance to the list of moths that are now gone or disappearing from Britain:

Bedworth Heath, New Cross, Allerton Bywater, Broad Lane, Armley Heights, Foggy Furze, Astley Bridge, Wilsden, Friern Barnet, Stow Hill, Barwell, Binley Woods, Brynglas House, Stanmore, Kilmaurs, Burley, Kinghorn, Old Monkland, Eggbuckland, Tothill.

* * *

As the winter wore on, an old pattern flared up: I couldn't sleep. A few days of restlessness passed, then a week, until the sleeplessness became full-blown insomnia. November plodded by in a dull haze, as did December and January, and then, by February, I realised I was entering new territory. Whenever I had experienced insomnia before, it usually lasted for a couple of weeks. Now, it seemed like a default condition, as if the border between sleep and wakefulness had been shut. From time to time, I would be granted the bliss of unconsciousness, but, even then, sleep was fragmented and dreamless, so that I woke up feeling as tired as before.

Gradually, I began retreating from the world, withdrawing from social encounters, allowing correspondences to go unanswered, ignoring text messages from friends. The most basic tasks had become a slog, while the very thought of sleep – or rather its impossibility – stimulated anxiety and dread. My partner helped as best she could, but nothing we tried, daily exercise, a change in diet, prescription medicine, seemed to work. The days and nights dragged by. The border remained closed.

I knew what the problem was, at least in part. It was a job that was leaving me chronically behind with deadlines, emails and administrative tasks, and that had stopped feeling manageable a long time ago. It was nothing special – many of my colleagues were in the same boat – but I suppose, too, that I had been absorbing something else during the last two years. For some time now, I had been reading or at least thinking about loss and extinction, first about the vanishing of the European eel, and now about the decline of British moth species, and perhaps some of the books and reports I had been reading were leaking into my being, accumulating in the body like trace metals. In any case, sleep was hard to come by that winter, and precisely when I needed rest, my body was refusing what would help it the most.

There was one particular night when, sitting in the kitchen, something happened. I don't quite know what to call it – perhaps it was a panic attack or a side-effect of chronic exhaustion – but I found myself struggling to breathe. My chest was unbearably tight, as if something heavy had been placed on my upper body, and I had the vivid sensation that the kitchen was shrinking, as if the walls were leaning towards the centre of the room. I remember closing my eyes, in order to steady myself and focus on my breathing. In my mind, though, I could still feel the room contracting, while the weight on my chest continued pressing down. I dug my fingers into my thighs and pushed my feet into the floor. *You'll be OK*, I said to myself, *just keep breathing*.

Eventually, the pressure on my chest eased off and my heart stopped fluttering. Then I realised how rigid my fingers were, and just this thought alone was helpful, since it allowed me to loosen them. During that whole episode, though, when my breathing was at its most constricted, I had been gripped by a terrible sensation – a feeling that still lingered even after the worst had passed.

It was the feeling of being trapped – trapped in the room, trapped in my body, trapped in the world – and of having no way out: a mind-reeling, body-panicking, holy-shit feeling of entrapment.

I have no idea what a moth feels – its experience is barred to us. A few days after that night in the kitchen, though, I began to wonder whether, from time to time, the experiences of others *are* available to us, in qualified fleeting glimpses. 'Don't anthropomorphise,' scientists tell us, and they are right, for the most part. We distort other animals by trying to conceive of them with our limited human sensorium – an apparatus which, try as it might, cannot grasp the specificity of other ways of being in the world. But what if, by adjusting our scales of vision, we could touch the far edge of another's experience, and what if we could feel our way from that edge to a possible centre? In the case of moths, that exercise would blind us, I think, for then we would feel the light burning in the skies, the fire-poisons spreading across the land, and the slow conflagration of home, and we would see how, for many moth species in Britain, the world is shrinking, is becoming less open and generous.

*   *   *

A few months after that night, I found myself in rural Devon with David. We were sitting in the pub, having just set our traps for the evening, when he began to tell me about an extraordinary event. It had happened to him last summer, a few weeks after I last saw him in Shropshire.

'I went for a walk on the beach,' David said, recalling a trip to the Kentish coast, where he sometimes goes moth-trapping. 'I was feeling a little cramped and wanted to stretch my legs. And then I saw the most remarkable thing. A stream of small white butterflies, flying in a more-or-less orderly line, coming straight over the Channel, from France.

'I couldn't believe what I was seeing. It was as though the butterflies were being reeled in on a fishing line. They were following each other, one by one, along the same path, and they just kept on coming. There must have been hundreds of them, travelling on a warm corridor of air.

'Then I did something I have never done before. I took my moth trap down to the beach that afternoon and placed it right there, next to the shoreline, exactly where the butter-flies first appeared over the land.'

David has been trapping since the 1960s – he has seen a lot of moths in his time. As he recounted his story, though, a sudden boyishness flashed across his face, so that I was given a glimpse of the fourteen-year-old schoolboy who set his first trap in his parents' garden in 1968, and who noted his first finds in the same book he continues to use to this day.

'I was full of adrenalin,' he said, continuing his story. 'I knew something interesting would come to the trap. There was a high-pressure system over Russia and an area of low-pressure in the Atlantic, and this meant that warm weather was moving to England from Southern Europe. A big migration was happening. The butterflies were a sign of it.

'So I stood on the beach, waiting for the sun to go down. Then I watched as the first moths started to appear – in fact, I stayed up all night. And when this one flew into the trap, I knew that it was special, something rare. But I wasn't prepared for what I saw. It was the feline moth – the *Cerura erminea*. And to my knowledge this was the first time it had ever appeared in mainland Britain. It had come to Kent on the same warm corridor of air that had carried the butterflies I had seen that afternoon.'

David traps most nights, even in the dead of winter. He has only missed a few nights since 1968, because of weddings, funerals and the occasional holiday. Still, after all these years, evenings spent setting the traps, followed by mornings spent observing and then releasing his night-haul of creatures – thousands upon thousands of such mornings and evenings – he was coming across unlikely discoveries, his eyes still widening before the tiny beings venturing his way. The night flights of moths continued to astonish him, to startle him out of himself, and after finishing his story, he leaned back in his chair, took a sip of beer, and closed his eyes for a moment, wearing an expression I can only describe as a state of bliss. And later that evening, as I imagined David standing on the beach that night, watching the moths appear from the sea, I had the sudden thought that this is what it is like, to live at this moment, a time of loss and extinction, but also of delight and encounter, a time late in history, yet still new to wonder. We bought another round and moved on to other topics: the rivalry between Arsenal and Tottenham, the controversial introduction of goal-line technology, and whether Liverpool might win the title that year.

*   *   *

A cloudy evening in April, a few weeks after my meeting with David. I have come out to inspect the moth trap. It is the first time we have trapped since the winter and I am surprised by how many have already appeared: a few Setaceous Hebrew Characters, some Silver Ys and a Lesser-bordered Yellow Underwing. Looking into the box, though, I can already sense that this first night will also be the last. I cannot explain why, but something in me wants to stop trapping, at least for now. In the morning, I will return the trap to the attic or perhaps loan it to a friend.

I stand in the garden while listening to the rumblings of traffic by our house. The last two months have been kind – I have been able to sleep again, have been able to drift off into that blessed realm – and later that night, for the first time in many months, I would be going to the cinema with a friend. A bus trundles by, bright windows briefly visible above the back wall, and then, after it pulls away, a moth appears in the corner of the garden. It circles the lamp, finds its way into the box, and then clings to the side of the wall. I kneel down and observe it. Its antennae are trembling, as though feeling the night for some kind of information, and its dark brown wings are slightly worn. It twitches and becomes still again, spasms, and then becomes still, and as I watch it crawl towards an egg carton, I am left with a feeling which is a little like wonder and a little like grief. How easy it is to step into this, I think, to lower oneself into the depths of this life, but how easy to miss it, too, to neglect the pull and charge of this place, this earth.

MUSSEL

In the summer of 1992, a man called Marek Vahula walked into a river and peered at the stones near his feet. A biology student, Vahula was completing research for his bachelor thesis – a study of the freshwater pearl mussels of the Pudisoo, a small river in northern Estonia. But what he came across that day was a scene of devastation: scores of dead mussels, lying in jagged heaps along the riverbed. Bewildered, he gathered the creatures from the river, placed them in his rucksack, and took them to the University of Tartu, where he was a student.

Vahula had visited at a strange time. Earlier that winter, tonnes of soil had tumbled into the river after a heavy spell of rain, slipping loose from a stretch of the Pudisoo riverbank that had been damaged by engineering works. The soil darkened the water, moving in thick billows downstream, and when it eventually reached a colony of pearl mussels, it smothered their shells, clogged their siphons, and killed them.

Not long after taking them back to Tartu, Vahula sent the mussels to the Stockholm Museum of Natural History.

There the specimens were examined by a group of scientists, among them Harry Mutvei, who had developed a precise method for calculating the age of these creatures.

The method was simple. First, you prepare a cross-section of the mussel's shell, cutting vertically from the umbo (the oldest part of the creature) to the shell's edge. Then you place the cross-section in a glutaraldehyde solution, a fixative agent that reacts with calcium. After being immersed in the liquid, thin delicate lines will eventually appear on the shell's surface, running from umbo to edge. These are rings of calcium, grown darker after contact with the solution, and each was laid down during a winter season.

For those who know how to interpret them, these rings contain many secrets: the chemical make-up of the mussel's environment, information about the temperature of historic summers, as well as periods when the mussel flourished or endured privation. They also reveal the mussel's age. By counting the rings – or the 'winter lines', as they are sometimes called – you can revisit each winter of the creature's life, and in 1992, as he counted these lines, Mutvei discovered something incredible. The mussels Vahula had sent his way were old, very old. Some were in their eighties, others in their nineties, while a handful exceeded the century mark, including a mussel born a hundred and twenty years earlier. But there was an even older creature in the collection – the greatest Estonian elder of them all. If Mutvei's tally of winter lines was right – and there is no reason to doubt his findings – this mussel was 134 years old, meaning it would have been born sometime in 1858.

True, much older animals have been identified. In 2006, researchers studying the Icelandic seabed came across a species of clam, *Arctica islandica*, that had reached the grand age of 507. And in 2016, a Greenland shark was found to be approximately 392 years old. We also know that some glass sponges in the Antarctic Ocean started life over a thousand years ago, while a species of deep-sea coral in the Gulf of Mexico, *Leiopathes glaberrima*, is over 2,000 years old.

Still, the Estonian mussel had lived through its fair share of history. When it began filtering the waters of the Pudisoo in 1858, Napoleon III had been Emperor of France for six years, and in 1870, when his reign came to an end, the mussel was beginning its teenage years. It entered its twenties during the First Boer War, its late thirties at the start of the Cuban War of Independence, and turned forty-two during the Paris Exposition of 1900. At the founding of the League of Nations in 1920, the mussel was sixty-two years old, and when Libya liberated itself from Italian rule, it was in its nineties. And as these events took place – as Mao led the Communist Revolution in China, as the first vaccine for polio was developed in the US, and as Margaret Thatcher came to power in Britain – the mussel kept growing.

And then, in the winter of 1991 or 1992 – after the Cold War had ended and after Estonia had gained independence from the Soviet Union – the mussel released its ancient grip on rock. For days something about the water had not been right – the light had been too grainy, the water too silty – and the creature keeled over and died.

When it was eventually sent to a scientist in Sweden, the mussel was cut open and placed under a microscope. And as Mutvei tallied up the rings on the shell – sixty-one, sixty-two, sixty-three – one can only imagine the excitement he must have felt when he reached seventy, then eighty, then ninety, an excitement that must have tipped into wonder when he passed a hundred and at last disbelief when he reached one hundred and twenty.

And he kept on counting – one hundred and thirty, one hundred and thirty-one – only stopping when he reached one hundred and thirty-four.

* * *

In his *Ecclesiastical History of the English People*, the Venerable Bede writes of an island in the ocean 'formerly called Albion'. Blessed with many riches, the island 'excels for grain and trees', is endowed with 'plenty of land' and is 'remarkable also for rivers abounding in fish', including 'the greatest plenty of salmon and eels'. It also has 'salt and hot springs', deep seams of 'copper, iron, lead, and silver', as well as a form of coal known as 'jet', a 'black and sparkling' rock which 'glitter[s] at the fire'. And because of the island's northerly latitude, the night skies are full of 'light in summer' – light that lingers so long that, even at midnight, 'the beholders are often in doubt whether the evening twilight still continues'.

I first read Bede's history after it was recommended by a colleague. A medieval scholar, she had learned of my interest in eels and told me that the fish made a few curious appearances in Bede's text. When I began to read the book, though, what struck me most about Bede's account were not the eels but his reference to a creature I knew very little about: a mussel. In a passage describing the island's many whales, dolphins and seals, Bede also writes of another watery animal – a shellfish – 'in which are often found excellent pearls of all colours'. The pearls are 'mostly white', he continues, but can also be 'red, purple, violet, and green'.

When I came across this passage, I thought Bede had strayed into the realm of myth. I had known of pearl-bearing oysters, but I had never heard of pearl-bearing mussels, and anyway, if such a thing was possible, wouldn't the pearls be white? But it did not take long to learn that the creature Bede was referring to was real. He was describing the freshwater pearl mussel, known by scientists as *Margaritifera margaritifera*. Nor did it take long to find out that, in Bede's time, such mussels could be found in most fast-flowing rivers in Britain, from Cornwall to Caithness. And what Bede had said was true: although they were mostly white, the pearls could take on all manner of colours, from light grey and dark brown to salmon pink and mulberry red. At one point in its history, Britain's rivers were literally strewn with pearls.

I began reading about mussels, borrowing books from the library and searching out scientific articles online. And before long a cairn of mussel-related texts began growing on my desk, among them dense monographs on molluscs, various issues of the *Journal of Conchology* and stacks of articles on mussel evolution. In time, the cairn migrated to the living-room bookcase, where it spread across one and then two shelves, a process my partner watched with bemused interest and then mild despair. She had seen me go through my earlier obsessions with eels and moths and understood what was happening to me now. Who knew where this would end up?

*   *   *

There is an intricate dance that goes on between mussels and rivers. The river offers the mussel the possibility of life – a home on the riverbed, as well as nourishment in the form of food and oxygen – while the mussel returns the river its clarity. Supreme drinkers, a single creature can filter up to fifty litres of water a day, while a hundred-strong colony of mussels, such as one might find along a healthy patch of river, will filter many thousands.

For the mussel, the filtering is also a form of feeding. As it draws water from a river, bits of organic material are caught in its gills, which are gradually taken into its body and absorbed by its digestive system. Among the particles it digests are phytoplankton, the mussel's main source of food, but the gills also take in silt, algae, bacteria and heavy metals. And because the mussels are constantly drinking and digesting, the filtering never stops. The creatures are turbo-charged micro-pumps, powered by the oxygen they draw from the water and fed by the river that they cleanse in return.

Really, though, this dance between river and mussel is a village-wide ceilidh, since an entire biotic community benefits from this relationship. By bringing lucidity to its world, the mussel allows light to reach the bottom of the river, which in turn powers the lives of submerged aquatic plants. The plants provide food for shrimp, snails, minnows and scores of insects, and because mussels excrete their faeces on the riverbed, they not only ensure that these aquatic plants have light, but that they are properly fertil-ised too. The faeces are also eaten by insect larvae, among them mayflies and caddisflies, and because of the complex clusters mussels can form on a riverbed, their shells provide shelter for other invertebrate species. Voracious dinner guests, mussels drink deeply from the sources of life. But they are also good hosts, creatures who know how to return the generosity that has been shown to them.

Mussels have also drawn our species into their dance. For many of our ancient ancestors, they offered a ready source of food, rich gobbets of protein that could be eaten raw or cooked over a fire. In South Africa, a 'mega midden' known as Mussel Point measures some 350 metres long and 200 metres wide, and similar shell heaps have been

found in Denmark, Portugal, France, Senegal and Brazil.
Indeed, such is the scale of some of these finds that some
archaeologists now argue that shellfish 'may have been a
critical food source to the survival of [early] human populations', with one hypothesis suggesting that, by exploiting
the shellfish of Africa's north-eastern coastlines, modern
humans found a coastal route 'out of Africa via the Red
Sea coast'. Even as they have satisfied our appetites, though,
propping up our diets when terrestrial food sources may
have been scarce, mussels have also fired our imaginations.
Around the world, archaeologists have unearthed the most
varied finds carved from mother-of-pearl – the iridescent
inner lining of mussels and oysters – including Mesolithic
buttons, Neolithic beads, and pendants from the Copper
Age. In Bulgaria, a terracotta figure dating back to 5,000
BCE was discovered near the village of Dolnoslav, its
unblinking eyes capped with mother-of-pearl.

The richness of our relationship with these animals is
partly reflected in our nomenclature. In North America, the
creatures go by any number of vernacular names, including
pigtoe and wartyback, heelsplitter and fatmucket, pistolgrip
and snuffbox. There are also Golden Orbs and Winged
Floaters, Southern Hickorynuts and Slippershells mussels,
not to mention Fluted Shells and Salina Muckets. Compared
to their American cousins, the freshwater mussels of Britain
are rather demurely named. The UK is home to six native
species, among them the Duck Mussel, the Painter's Mussel,
the Swan Mussel and the Freshwater Pearl Mussel, and

although this last species lacks the inspired lyricism of its American counterparts, it is unique in being the only freshwater creature to bear those tiny orbs we know as pearls. Composed of crystallised calcium carbonate, the pearls form when parasites or particles of sediment enter the mussel's shell, to which it responds by secreting a substance known as nacre – the same material with which it lines its inner shell. The pearls are thus dazzling responses to stress, lustrous answers to the shock of being alive.

In the early twentieth century, you could search the bed of a fast-flowing river in Britain and stand a decent chance of finding a freshwater pearl mussel. Today, only a handful of British rivers are clean enough for these animals to reproduce and thrive. An extremely sensitive species, the mussels are vulnerable to the slightest changes in their environment, and as more rivers are impacted by pollution, over-abstraction and sewage discharge, as well as the effects of upland farming and deforestation, the conditions that sustain their lives have become increasingly rare. The situation is much the same across Central Europe, where the population has sunk by 95 per cent. Once abundant in rivers from Ireland to Russia, pearl mussels have disappeared from most of their former range, and even in places where they are found, their existence is often a ghostly one. The mussels can only reproduce in rivers that meet their strict requirements, which means that, even where colonies endure, they are simply living out the end of their days – a dying generation unreplenished by new life.

These are mussels for whom the world is not damaged enough to kill them off completely, but also not clean enough to offer them a future.

The more I learned about these animals, the more they deepened a realisation that had been steadily growing in recent years. It wasn't just the fact that everything is connected – often in ways too intricate for us to understand. It was the recognition that we are sustained by our relationships with each other and that these relationships literally make us what we are. For what is an eel without its wetlands, and without the worms and snails it subsists upon? And what is a moth without the plants that 'host' it as a caterpillar, or the microorganisms that help to build the soil in which those plants grow? From this perspective, what we call an 'eel' or a 'moth' is a convenient taxonomic abstraction, a way of isolating single lines in the web of life. But since these lines are completely dependent upon and entangled with the lines of countless others, there really is no such thing as an individual. There are only trillions of kinds of relationships; only countless ingenious ways of dwelling in a shared world.

Exchange, interdependency, community – these too are at the heart of the mussel's relationship with its world and among the things I found so compelling about this species. The mussels were proof of the most beautiful truth – one you could literally touch if you held one of their shiny pearls: we are here thanks to the gifts of others and the gift of life itself.

I continued reading about the species, seeking out more books and articles, and one evening I came across news of an exciting project – a conservation scheme in the Highlands. Led by Scottish Natural Heritage, the project aimed at safeguarding the region's populations of pearl mussels, an effort that involved repairing miles of riverbed habitat and working with local farmers to prevent downstream pollution. It also involved removing river obstructions that were causing erosion or 'scour', planting trees along riverbanks, as well as working with environmental agencies to protect the species from illegal fishing. In 2016, a freshwater conservationist found 113 dead mussels by a Scottish riverbank, the shells ransacked for their pearls and then carelessly tossed aside.

Shortly after learning about the project, I got in touch with Scottish Natural Heritage. I wanted to know more about the conservation scheme and to learn how mussels were doing in Britain, and soon I received an email from a freshwater biologist. We corresponded for a few weeks, during which time I borrowed maps of the Highlands, finger-tracing the edges of towns, mountains and rivers. I had lived in Britain for eleven years now, but had never been north of Manchester, and the more I studied the maps, the more I could feel the pricklings of wanderlust in my feet. The Easter holidays were only a few weeks away, the bus trip was affordable, and perhaps, if he could be persuaded, the biologist might show me a stretch of river where some mussels lived, so that I could see for myself these creatures in 'which are often found excellent pearls of all colours'.

* * *

Iain Sime is a tall, quietly spoken Scotsman. When we meet one morning in April, in the light-filled lobby of Scottish Natural Heritage, just outside Inverness, he has been busy with phone calls, emails and meetings. 'Death by spreadsheet,' he says with a wry smile, gesturing towards his office. 'Anyway, it's good that you're here. I don't visit the field as much as I used to.'

On the day we meet, Iain has arranged for us to visit a large estate north of Inverness. He wants to show me a stretch of river where, unknown to the local residents, a colony of pearl mussels is thriving. But we have trouble leaving his office. The vehicle he has booked for the day, an electric car owned by Scottish National Heritage, defeats us. There is no ignition for the key, and the cockpit looks more like the interior of a spaceship than a car. We prod helplessly at a few buttons, eliciting strange beeps from the dashboard, and then Iain throws up his hands and walks back to his office. He returns moments later with a grin and tells me that we had been trying too hard – all the car needed was a little pressure on the brake. He tries again, and soon we are pulling out of the driveway.

'Pearl fishing is still a problem,' Iain says, as he begins to tell me about the river we are visiting, which he has asked me not to name. 'We get reports all the time. Huge spoils by the river, dead mussels piled up on the bank. It's a terrible waste, really. Someone can kill hundreds of mussels before finding a single pearl. But the colony I'm showing you isn't on any official map. The estate owners know about these mussels, and maybe one or two locals, but we're trying to keep it a secret for now.'

The colony has placed Scottish Natural Heritage in a tricky position. If Iain and his colleagues applied for official designation, then the river – and by extension the mussels – would be protected by special environmental laws. However, the colony's existence would then become public knowledge, and if certain people caught wind of this, it could be disastrous for the mussels. Although pearl mussels are an officially protected species, and although killing, harming or disturbing them is a crime, they continue to be raided by fishers looking to sell the pearls on the black market.

'Anyway,' Iain says, 'we still haven't figured out what to do. At the moment, the mussels don't have any formal protection. But it's possible that might change before too long.'

When I ask Iain about the pearl fishing, he tells me about some of the damage he has seen. Huge cairns of lifeless mussels, their shells snapped open at the hinge. A whole colony uprooted from their river and dumped on the grass. He sighs as he talks, seemingly more saddened than shocked, but then, when he begins talking about some of the old fishers he has met over the years, I notice that his tone softens. The traditional fishers, he says, knew how to fish in a sustainable way. They knew which mussels were likely to bear pearls, and which were not – and they always left the latter untouched. And when mussel populations began declining in the 1980s, Iain tells me that the traditional fishers were also the first to press for legislative protection. Unlike their maverick counterparts – those chancers who hoped to strike it lucky over a couple of days' fishing – the old fishers cared for the rivers in which they worked. And at a time when there was little public concern for mussels, they made sure that as many people as possible heard the alarm. Today, the species is protected under the Wildlife and Countryside Act, which means that you can only search for them in rivers if you have an official licence.

I ask Iain about the chancers, and he tells me about a famous incident that occurred in 1967.

'That was when a well-known fisher called Bill Abernathy found a huge pearl in the River Tay. He sold it to a jeweller in Perth, who bought it for some undisclosed amount, and though Abernathy never found such a big pearl again, he didn't need to. That pearl made him a very rich man.

'But the problem,' Iain continues, 'is that it started a gold rush – or rather a pearl rush. People read about Abernathy in the papers and saw an easy way to make money. And they began coming up to the rivers over the weekend, looking for pearls and leaving big spoils behind. A few got lucky, I'm sure, but it was devastating for the mussels.'

I look out the window. For the last few miles we have been driving through open farmland and now we are turning off the main road onto a smaller lane. After another mile, we drive over a narrow stone bridge and then follow the road until it ends at the corner of a large rapeseed field.

'This is it,' Iain says, parking the car. He pulls out a few things from the boot: a map of the area, a GPS tracker, two pairs of waist-high waders, and two orange bathyscopes. 'That's the fancy name,' he says, handing one to me. 'We just call them glass-bottom buckets.'

We sling the waders over our shoulders and skirt the edge of the field. A tractor rumbles along the path before us, and the air is tinted yellow by the rapeseed flowers. We walk for a few hundred metres, and then, after stopping by an oak tree, Iain consults his map, presses a few buttons on his GPS tracker, and points to a hill thick with brambles and hawthorn. 'There,' he says, 'the mussels are on the other side.' We crouch down, push our way through the undergrowth, and then emerge through a hawthorn-framed gap. A river meets us on the other side, its gleaming length moving quickly down the valley.

I don't know what I am expecting, but it isn't quite this. The place doesn't seem distinguished in any special way, at least to my eyes. There are some overgrown fields by the far bank, some scraggly trees by a hill, and an outcrop of grey rocks in the middle of the river. It looks like an ordinary river, and certainly not the stronghold of a species that has vanished from most of Europe.

We take off our shoes, slip into our waders, and then I watch as Iain climbs down the bank and wades into the river. When I try to follow, I immediately slip on the wet rocks. Iain is fifty feet away by the time I regain my balance, peering through his bathyscope.

I walk upstream and brace myself against the river's push. By leaning towards the water, I find that the current will support me, and after finding the knack of it, I place my bathyscope on the river's surface and look down. For a moment all I can see is an orange tunnel of light, and at the end of that tunnel the water's white churn. But then the instrument steadies in my hand, sight clarifies, and a world leaps into vision: small forests of algae, their fronds splayed out like hair in a bathtub; glimmers of yellow rock against dark stone; and a highway of cold water, streaked with hundreds of bits of flashing sediment. I look down, moving upstream in silence, and every so often, when the current tilts my balance, the river at the end of the scope disappears, to be replaced by a turbulent cloud of white water. When I find my feet once more, the river-picture weaves itself together again, the white swirl parting to reveal dark rocks and the algae's languid waving fronds.

'Here!' Iain shouts, lifting his hand. 'Have a look at this!'

I wade upstream, and when I am alongside Iain I look down too. 'Can you see them?' he asks. 'I'm pointing to them with my boot.'

I angle my bathyscope towards Iain's feet but see nothing – just a cluster of rocks on a bed of gravel. The rocks are of various shades – grey, black, yellow – but there are no mussels.

'Keep looking,' Iain says.

I look again. The same sight, the same set of rocks – but now, under the pressure of Iain's suggestion, a subtle transformation occurs, as though an underwater light had been switched on. There it is – wedged between two small stones – its shell now clearly visible – a pearl mussel! And there – yet another – its white gills moving slowly in the water – and there – two more! – their shells gleaming darkly above the stones. Rows of mussels standing quietly in gravel, upright in shafts of sun. Filtering water, pointing towards the sky.

'Those are its siphons,' Iain says, anticipating my first question.

Along the edge of one of the mussels, we can see two frilly apertures. One of them is an 'inhalant' siphon, Iain tells me, while the other is an 'exhalant' siphon. The former enables the mussel to extract organic particles from the river for digestion, while the latter allows the mussel to discharge newly clarified water into the river. The siphons quiver in the current as Iain talks: two small vents that open onto the darkness of the mussel's interior.

'These are a good age,' he continues. 'I reckon around thirty years or so.'

He reaches down, plucks a creature from the bed, and brings it to the surface in a shower of water. 'If you're quick,' he says, turning the mussel over in his hand, 'you can see the foot it uses to attach itself to the riverbed.' He points at its lower edge, where the mussel is slightly ridged, but the foot has already retracted. All we can see is its dark shell, silvered here and there with beads of water.

Iain hands me the mussel, which feels snug and cool against the hand. It is heavier than I had anticipated, and when I turn it over, I notice a hint of gold towards its tapered end, which Iain tells me is a remnant of the mussel's earlier self. During its first months of life, he says, the mussel is encased in a bright yellow shell, and although it spins a much darker shell for itself as it ages, the kernel of its infant years endures, like a kind of birthmark. Whatever age they reach, their shells will always retain this golden core.

I continue turning the creature in my hand, and as I do waves of iridescence begin running across its wet surface. I pass the mussel back to Iain, who kneels down, tenses against the river's surge and places it carefully between two rocks. Later that day, the mussel will reach out with its foot, realign itself in the water, and then clasp onto the riverbed, where it might stay for the next fifty or sixty years.

We retrace our steps along the river, this time with the current at our backs. And now, as I look through my bathyscope, it occurs to me that some of the stones beneath us are not stones but mussels, and that stretches of the riverbed are alive. We proceed slowly, head down, vision beguiled by the waters.

'Now this is interesting,' Iain says, when we return to the bend of river where we first started. 'Have a look at this.'

I steady the bathyscope and look down. Beside our feet are a clutch of mussels, perhaps five or six of them, and swimming above the mussels are two small fish. 'Brook lampreys,' Iain says, before drawing my attention to a tiny row of perforations along the necks of the fish, which he tells me are breathing holes. We observe the drama for a while – the lampreys hovering above the mussels, the mussels glinting darkly in the water – and as we do another small fish appears, its creamy flanks dappled with small brown dots. Iain says that it's a baby trout, one of the mussels' host fish.

As we look at the fish with our bathyscopes, Iain describes the mussel's life cycle, and the particular – and peculiar – things that must happen for this animal to reproduce. And though I had read about this before, in the books I had amassed at home, it was still strange to hear it spoken out loud.

Every spring and summer, male mussels release their sperm into the river in a random spray of fertility. Some of this sperm finds its way to female mussels, who, in the process of filter feeding, draw the sperm into their bodies and use it to fertilise their eggs. Once this is done, the female mussels eject millions of larvae known as glochidia, and remarkably this seems to be a synchronised event, with most of the females in any given river releasing their larvae on the same day. Swirling in the water, some of the larvae then clasp onto the gills of passing juvenile trout and salmon, and if they find purchase there, they will grow on the fish's gills for the next several months. Millions of larvae won't find a host, Iain tells me, and will quickly perish. And although millions more *will* find a host, they will be deposited in the wrong kind of riverbed – where there is too much silt, for example, or where the flow of the river is too slow. These eventually die too. But for those that find the optimum conditions, there is every chance they will survive into adulthood, like those we had just seen. These are the mussels that filter hundreds of litres of water every week, purifying the river of sediments, algae and bacteria. All this is only possible, however, because of the salmon and the trout, who not only host the glochidia for those crucial early months, but who also ferry them *upstream*, against the river's flow. And so the creatures help dance each other into existence. Without the fish, the mussels would eventually be washed into the sea, just as, without the mussels cleaning the water, the river-beds would be much less hospitable to the fish.

As Iain talks, the lampreys swim away, followed by the trout. I lift my head from the scope, as though turning away from a dream. The path by the river is still there, as is the overgrown field on the river's far side. Now, though, everything seems a little clearer and more defined.

'Red kite,' Iain says, pointing up. Above us, outstretched wings turn slowly above treetops, wing-tips illuminated by sun, and for a moment I have a fleeting apprehension of the tiers extending above and below. The kite in its upper world, the humans below, and the mussels in the fast-flowing river; a varied and glorious skein of life.

We climb the bank and look back over the river. Without our bathyscopes, the water's surface has become dark and impenetrable again, opaque to human eyes. As we stand there, though, I think of how, just a few minutes ago, I had waded towards the river's centre, tilted my scope towards the riverbed, and caught sight of a hundred dark and gleaming things: stones, gravel, algae, trout and, further away, half-buried in a gravel bed, what I thought was the outline of a juvenile mussel, a golden shell glistening at depth.

We sit on the bank and unpeel our waders. We have only spent an hour in the water, exploring a small run of river no more than twenty metres long, yet it feels as though we have travelled for miles. I look up, hoping to catch another glimpse of those outstretched wings – but the kite has gone. We climb the hillock, make our way through hawthorn and bramble, then walk along a path until we reach an electric car standing by a yellow field.

* * *

Walking in the river that day with Iain, awake to the cold surge of water against my body, I had never felt so sure that the world was alive, that the water and the rocks were alive, and that the river was a living, breathing thing. And seldom have I seen so clearly with my own eyes how delicately and exactly things were connected: river and mussel, mussel and fish, water and life. I came away from that trip with a renewed sense of life's deep pools and glittering marvels, and for weeks, too, I felt a lingering sense of bewilderment and wonder. For how strange it is – how utterly strange – that we find ourselves alive in a world of mussels and trout and red kites – creatures whose appearance on Earth we could have easily missed by millions of years. And how strange, too, that it has all emerged on this unlikely orb, which, with its exact proximity to the sun, its stabilising companion of a moon, and its precise composition of atmospheric gases, is the most outlandish pearl of all.

At the same time, I have never felt the tragedy of our situation so deeply. The Highland river we stepped into was a place of marvels: a trout-filled, lamprey-crowded, life-rich world. Increasingly, though, it is a kind of river that is disappearing from Britain and Europe: one clean enough to bear pearls. 'They're losing their character,' Iain had said to me, as we drove back to his office near Inverness. He was talking about the rivers of Britain and how profoundly they have changed in recent decades. Because of deforestation in the uplands, more silt was tumbling into our watercourses, which was changing the sedimentation load of river currents. And because synthetic fertilisers were leaching into catchments from intensively farmed fields, the chemical composition of rivers was also changing – a problem compounded by over-abstraction, sewage discharge and other forms of pollution. All around the country, mussels were being untenanted from their homelands, and it was an uprooting being experienced by other animals too, with a thousand terrible variations.

A few weeks after returning to Bristol, I began to write up my notes from Scotland, and as I did so I found myself picking up a book called *The Gift*, Lewis Hyde's distinctive account of the various meanings of gifts and gift-giving. First given to me in 2004 as a graduation present from my high school teacher, it is one of the books I have returned to most often in my life, and from which I have drawn much encouragement and inspiration. After that trip to Inverness, though, the book took on a new depth. Passages underlined many years ago flashed with new meanings, and I began to understand – or, rather, to *feel* – something that I had grasped intellectually before, but which I now felt in the gut. *The world itself is a kind of gift – the best and strangest of them all; and yet gifts can only survive if they are treated as such.* In their own way, that is what the mussels were telling us, and it is a message that we urgently need to hear, not only for their sakes but for ours as well.

According to Hyde, a gift is characterised by the following features. First, it places its recipient in some kind of moral debt; second, it has an intrinsic desire to keep moving through the world; and finally, it changes shape as it moves from person to person, hand to hand. In all these aspects, gifts are fundamentally distinct from other kinds of property. When I buy a bicycle from a shop, for instance, I do not feel especially tied to the person who sold it to me. When I receive a gift, however, the giver and I become bound up in some way, even if their identity is unknown to me. And whereas a commodity is characterised by the inertia of ownership – the bicycle becomes my property when I buy it – a gift is governed by another tendency, namely the need to remain in circulation.

This momentum stems from a powerful fact. When we become recipients of a gift, our lives are not only enriched and enlarged, but we are also left with a feeling of gratitude. In turn, this gratitude activates a part of us generally left untouched by most forms of market exchange – a desire to 'earn' the generosity that has been shown to us. We want to be equal to the gift, to be worthy of it, and because a gift addresses us at this level, we often find ourselves moved to our own acts of kindness. In this way, generosity can be said to grow itself, as one gift leads to another, which leads to yet another.

But where might a gift begin and end? And how might we trace the expanding circles of its movement through the world? According to Hyde, the most common form of gift-giving occurs between two people, a reciprocal relationship he classifies as the simplest form of exchange.

But there is another form of gift-giving that unfolds on a much more expansive plane, what he calls 'circular giving'. In this form of giving, gifts do not go back and forth between one person and another, but instead move in a circle and in such a manner that no one ever receives from the same person to whom she gives. The entire mood of this gift-giving is different, Hyde argues. In such a relationship, I not only give to someone from who I do not receive, but my 'gift goes around a corner', passing out of my sight into a realm over which I have no control. In this kind of relationship, 'I have to give blindly', and so relinquish any personal attachment I might have to that gift. For that reason, I may also come to 'feel a sort of blind gratitude' – a thankfulness for all the gifts that pass around their own corners to me.

In its own way, what Iain and I witnessed in that Highland river was a kind of gift economy, one which unfolded on this more expansive plane. To the river's gift of life – the gift of food and water and oxygen – the mussel offered the gift of lucidity. And as a result of this relationship, other gifts emerged. By extracting sediments from the water, the mussel filtered the river for its neighbours, among them adult salmon and trout who require clean gravel beds to lay their eggs. In turn, the fish that eventually hatched from these eggs, and for whom the river acts as a nursery, engaged in their own acts of hospitality. These are the fish that, before swimming out to sea, unwittingly broadcast juvenile mussels on the riverbed, where, if the conditions are right, the creatures can grow for more than a hundred years.

Of course, this is an anthropocentric way of looking at these relationships. The animals involved are not knowingly engaging in acts of generosity, but simply trying to flourish by using all the capacities and mechanisms evolution has devised for them. Nevertheless, seeing their behaviour through the prism of the gift helps to clarify a basic truth, one that even the most anthropocentrism-averse scientists would agree upon: that nothing has its life alone, because existence is always shared. One word for this shared existence is 'ecology', and perhaps this is the most expansive plane of all: not the exchange of gifts between two people, or the movement of gifts within a human society, but the gift of life itself, which is made possible by a vast community of others, from microbes in the soil to the nutrient-recycling work of rivers. 'The only essential is this,' Hyde writes, '*the gift must always move*. There are other forms of property that stand still, that mark a boundary or resist momentum, but the gift keeps going.'

What would the world look like if reimagined – and lived – from the perspective of the gift economy? Of course, we would still need to till the earth and divert water from rivers to irrigate our crops. In all likelihood, we would also need some basic form of market exchange. Yet the whole manner in which we take from the natural world – or rather receive from it – would be different. Rather than consumers of resources, we would be participants in the community of life; and because we would not feel entitled to life's gifts, but rather indebted to and grateful for them, we would better acknowledge those things that enable our flourishing. As it stands, one of the great moral and imaginative failings of our dominant economic system is its inability to recognise the vibrant autonomy of other things. In a gift society, however, natural beings and processes have their own meaningful and independent life, and that recognition, quite apart from restraining us from excessive or inappropriate use, immerses us in a world of others, a world of gifts.

* * *

It is late June, two months after my trip to Scotland, and I am standing on a ferry with my friend Holly in the middle of Windermere, England's largest lake. We left Bristol earlier that morning – Thermoses filled with coffee, sky streaked with dawn light – and will soon be meeting a conservationist called Louise Lavictoire. For now, though, we are simply enjoying the sunshine, our faces prickled by the wind coming off the water. In the middle distance, two small boats are crossing the lake, listing ever so slightly as they go.

I had a feeling that Holly would be interested in this trip. A poet from Bristol, she has a fascination with shells and watery creatures, and when I asked if she would like to see a special laboratory in Cumbria, where freshwater biologists were rearing thousands of juvenile mussels, she wrote back straight away. 'When can we go?'

We reach the other side of the lake and step off the ferry. The place we are looking for is just around the corner from the pier, and before long we are walking up a driveway towards a large stone building. A sign at the entrance reads 'FBA: The Freshwater Biological Association', and as we stand at the front door, contemplating whether we should enter or wait outside, we are met by a woman carrying a crate full of jars.

'Oh,' she says, 'you must be the Bristol folk. Come on in. I'm Heather – Louise is waiting for you upstairs.'

We follow Heather into a dark hallway, passing a series of glass cabinets on our left. The cabinets are filled with old microscopes, antique barometers and glass vials, and when I squint at a small caption, I learn that one of the vials contains a water sample taken from Lake Titicaca in the 1930s. We climb a staircase, walk past a few offices, and soon we are standing in a book-crammed meeting room where Louise is waiting for us. Along one side of the room, a large window frames a glinting view of the lake.

The proximity of water seems fitting, given the nature of the institute's work. But as Louise hands out mugs of tea, we learn that it is not without its dangers. She tells us that several years ago, Storm Desmond raised the level of the lake by several feet and that the floodwaters spilled into the building's basement and ground floors. Hundreds of books were waterlogged, including rare scientific monographs on freshwater biology, some of which were damaged beyond repair. 'We had to dehumidify the books using a special machine,' Louise says. 'It was very expensive.'

We settle into our chairs and cradle our tea. Thick curtains of rain have begun advancing across the lake, blotting out the land beyond the bay, and as the windows fog up with the warmth of our bodies, I have the sudden impression of being out at sea. Then Louise begins telling us about the project she oversees, a captive breeding programme for mussels.

'It started in 2007, when we began collecting mussels from English rivers. The mussels were then brought here and placed in special tanks. As you know, most English rivers aren't healthy enough for these mussels to reproduce in the wild. So what we've effectively created here is a nursery, a place which mimics their river environments and where mussels can breed and grow.'

As Louise tells us more about the breeding programme, we learn that her project is occasionally referred to as 'The Ark', and that it was established with both the worst fears and best hopes in mind. The fear was that England's remaining mussel colonies could easily become extinct in our lifetimes. For the last mussels to disappear, she explains, all that was needed was a few years of bad floods or some toxic spills in their catchments. The breeding programme was therefore a rear-guard measure, a way of preserving, in case of some catastrophe, a genetic bank of the country's indigenous mussels.

And the hope, Holly asks?

'Well,' Louise says, 'what we're doing here is important – raising the mussels, ensuring as much genetic diversity as possible. But if we really want the mussels to do well, we have to work on a much larger scale. We have to restore entire rivers, entire ecosystems.' She looks out the window and pauses. 'I suppose the real hope is that our work will eventually be redundant, because the mussels will be able to flourish on their own. At the moment, though, they can't survive in most of our rivers. The females are still releasing their glochidia, but because there are fewer mussels, and because salmon and trout stocks have also declined, fewer juveniles are reaching maturity.'

There are other problems too. In the last ten years, the organisations tasked with protecting England's wildlife and ecosystems have been stripped to the bone by years of relentless austerity. Since the breeding programme was first established, the Environment Agency has lost nearly two-thirds of its budget, while Natural England has lost half its funding and shed a thousand environmental inspectors. And since these institutions were among the funders of Louise's institute, it made her day-to-day work much harder and more uncertain.

'Every penny we receive – and we don't receive that much – is counted and scrutinised. And I worry that, maybe a few years from now, the money will simply dry up.

'Anyway,' she says, gathering up our mugs, 'would you like to see the mussels? It looks like the rain has passed.'

We follow Louise out of the building, where the car park has been washed clean by rain. On the other side of the road is a tall, padlocked gate, and after Louise opens it, we step into a large courtyard. Along one side of the courtyard is a wooden shed, signed 'Pearl Mussel HQ', and after passing the shed we come across dozens of large circular tanks.

Peering into one of them, we see a swirl of dark shapes. 'Juvenile salmon,' Louise says, as our eyes adjust to the movements of the fish.

She touches a long grey pipe that connects the tank to an adjoining one. 'As you probably know by now, mussels need salmon and trout to host their glochidia, and so we've tried to replicate that relationship here. The glochidia are placed in their own tank, gradually make their way to the fish tank via the pipe, and then, after swirling around the water, some will be lucky enough to latch onto the gills of the salmon.

'The salmon don't really like the glochidia,' Louise continues. 'They're a kind of irritant for them and they react by growing a layer of skin over the larvae, a process called "encystment". But of course, that's what the mussels are after. The cyst forms a barrier over the glochidia – a protective wall – and this allows the glochidia to live on the fish for a few months. The glochidia then mature, and later, when the cyst flakes off, they are seeded onto the riverbed. They'll have grown quite big at this stage, and if they survive into adulthood, those crucial months with their host fish will have had everything to do with it.'

We move to another tank, this one filled with baby trout. Louise picks up a small net from the ground, scoops up one of the fish, and gently pulls back its gill cover.

'Can you see them?' she asks, motioning for us to come closer.

We stare into the rawness of the exposed gills, and there, scattered in small clusters, are tiny white spots. The spots look like braille marks or specks of sand.

'Glochidia,' Louise says, 'and quite a few of them too.'

She returns the trout to the tank, where it rejoins the dark fish-swirl. Then we walk to a nearby building, opening the door to a dim corridor echoing with the sound of trickling water. At the end of the corridor are white trays sitting on metal stands, and as we come closer we see that the trays are connected to an intricate system of hoses and tubes. Louise takes us to one of the trays, removes its plastic lid, and invites us to look down.

'Keep looking,' she says. 'They're a little hard to spot at first.'

When I look, all I can see is water and sand and gravel. But when Holly points to the corner of the tray, guiding my eyes to a small cluster of brown shapes, I begin to see them. Sitting at the bottom of the tray, and barely distinguishable from the gravel in form and colour, are a handful of tiny mussels, each no bigger than my thumbnail.

Now that our eyes are tuned to them, we begin to see them everywhere. Small beings gleaming softly in the water, their shells the colour of muddy gold. Little pebbles of life. A few have burrowed deep into the gravel beds, so that only the tips of their rims are visible, but others are out in the open, their bodies quivering slightly in the current, which is being generated by the piped-in water. When we look beneath the tray, we also see that two mussels have fallen into the drainage channel below. 'It happens all the time,' Louise says, scooping them up in her hands. She returns one of the mussels to the gravel bed and places the other in Holly's palm.

On Holly's hand, the mussel looks pitifully fragile and small. Its shell is pale yellow, darkened here and there with streaks of brown, although, when we hold it up to the light, it becomes translucent under the glare of the overhead lamps. It was a few months new to this world – and, given the chance, it might live for a hundred years.

Holly gives the mussel back to Louise, who places it on the gravel bed of the tray. There are several more trays to see, and as we walk past them, we notice that they have been labelled with the names of different rivers. These are rivers from which the adult mussels were collected, Louise says, and from which these juvenile mussels are descended. And they are being kept in separate trays because, having evolved in different rivers (which Louise asks us not to name), the mussels were genetically distinctive. Devon mussels are unlike their counterparts in Cornwall, which are different again from the mussels of Cumbria or Lancashire.

Louise's comment makes me pause. For months I had been lumping the creatures under a single term – the freshwater pearl mussel – but in fact the mussels are made up of numerous clans, with their own genealogies and family histories. Shaped by the rivers they had shaped in return, they were still evolving in their own ways, continuing the long journey that had started when they branched off from their mollusc ancestors millions of years ago. Yet when is a Cumbria mussel no longer from Cumbria, or a Devon mussel from Devon? The creatures in the tray had been rescued from compromised rivers and, thanks to the breeding programme, were being nurtured into adulthood under Louise and Heather's care. But having lived indoors their entire lives, they had never known a wild river in all its complexity and aliveness, which made me wonder about the labels on the tray. In what sense were the mussels really *from* these places? This building on the edge of Windermere was a shelter for them, a sanctuary from unforgiving environments, but it was also a world apart, removed from the homes of their ancestors.

'There's one more thing you might like to see,' Louise says, leading us down a hallway into another room. We enter a narrow office, where a large microscope sits on a table by the window.

At Louise's invitation, I sit at the microscope and squint into the lens. At first, it is hard to make anything out – the light is too bright. But as the shapes come into focus – a series of brown flakes against a silver-white background – the significance of what I am seeing becomes clear. These are mussels, dozens of baby mussels, magnified many times by the power of the microscope.

I stand up and trade places with Holly. And then I watch as she too becomes absorbed by the realm beneath the microscope.

'Aren't they amazing?' Louise asks. 'These ones are just a day or two old.'

After a few minutes, Holly stands up, looking a little dazed by what she's seen. 'They look like living sand,' she says, and when I sit down again, I find that her description is exactly right. Trembling under the viewfinder, the mussels looked like vibrating grains of life, animated specks of light.

For some time we continue observing the creatures, Holly and I taking turns at the microscope, and then reluctantly leave the room. The best of the day is behind us now, and if we are to make it back to Bristol that evening, we will soon have to go.

We walk out of the office and return to the car park. Louise has kindly offered to drive us to the railway station at Kendal, but first she wants to show us her local river, just a few miles away.

As we drive, my mind is filled with the things we have seen that day – the fish swirling in the tanks, the juvenile mussels in their white trays, the day-old mussels under the microscope. And I think, too, of one of the names of Louise's project, The Ark, and how precarious it was, susceptible to cuts in government funding, as well as vulnerable to storms and floods. The vision behind the programme was a hopeful one, since it was premised on the belief that, one day, the country's rivers might be healthy enough to sustain the lives of mussels. But the Ark was also a frail vessel on troubled seas, for who knew whether, in a country of degraded and dying rivers, the future would be spacious enough to accommodate its precious cargo. In the meantime, though, Louise had work to do: reports to write, funding to secure, mussels to breed.

I look out the window. Above us, someone has graffitied 'Make Ecocide Law' on a bridge over the road, and after taking the next junction, Louise drives us down a series of small roads, which eventually takes us to a stone bridge. We cross onto the other side, the river running dark and clear beneath us.

When we step out, it's to the sluice-rush of river in our ears. Slick grey rocks run up the length of the river, generating wedges of white foam against the water's flow, and as we stand there, a wagtail alights on one of the rocks. The river looks beautiful, its surface burnished with clear summer light, and yet, after our day at Louise's laboratory, it is hard not to think of how depleted it must be, and what chemicals were even then flowing past our feet. The wagtail bobs up and down, up and down, and we watch it while the river rushes past, hurtling towards the sea.

* * *

What would vanish from the world if pearl mussels became extinct? And what kind of disappearance might take place in rivers, as well as in us?

Before we had parted ways in Inverness, Iain had taken me to a small library in his office and reached for a book called *The Summer Walkers*. 'Read this,' he said, pressing the book into my hands, and for the rest of the afternoon, while he carried on with his work, I found myself in a different world. Written by Timothy Neat, the book offers a remarkable account of an old way of life – one it records without any hint of romanticism or nostalgia – and more than any other, it was this book that showed me the depth of the historical relationship between mussels and humans.

In 1996, Neat began interviewing members of Scotland's Travelling community. At the time, fewer than five thousand were 'living a traditional semi-nomadic lifestyle,' he writes, with fewer still 'living the old migratory lifestyle in bow-tents' – 'probably less than fifty'. The aim of *The Summer Travellers*, he explains, was to 'document aspects of that life' while they were 'still fresh in the minds of individuals who spent extended periods of their lives on the road'.

Among the Travellers Neat interviewed for his book were Eddie Davies and Essie Stewart, both pearl-fishers. Over a period of months, they told Neat many stories, recounting their many years of travelling the roads, camping beneath the stars, and fishing for pearls in dozens of Highland rivers. As I read these interviews,

I was introduced to a world I knew nothing about: the rich traditions of the Travellers, their songs, customs and folktales, as well as the various occupations of different families, from hawking and horse-dealing to tin-smithing and pearl-fishing. At the same time, Neat's book reaffirmed something I had learned in relation to eels and moths, but which was powerfully confirmed for me again: that the disappearance of a species is always a plural event, because it involves the unravelling of an interconnected world. In most cases, that unravelling happens for other species, often in ways that we do not fully understand: otters and bitterns are affected by the loss of eels, just as birds and bats suffer due to the loss of moths. In the case of mussels, that unmaking also extends to humans, or at least to the lives of the traditional pearl-fishers. And while this is not the primary reason we should care about extinction – since other animals have a value quite apart from their benefit to humans – the experience of the pearl-fishers might help us appreciate a basic truth: that the loss of one species is always a loss for others.

The son and grandson of pearl-fishers, Eddie Davies began working on rivers in the 1930s when he was five years old. He started fishing alongside his father, who also began his working life at a tender age, and would continue fishing until his back, twisted by more than sixty years of pearl-fishing, gave out in his early seventies. By the time he and Neat met, Eddie was living in Sutherland with his daughter Sandra, living on monthly disability cheques.

The woman whom Eddie would marry in 1969, Essie Stewart, was also brought up in a Travelling family. Abandoned at birth in 1941, Essie was adopted and raised by Mary Stewart, a member of the famous Stewart clan from Lairg, Sutherland. Mary's adoptive father was Ailidh Dall, reputed to be one of Scotland's greatest storytellers, and it was from him that Essie learned, in Gaelic, the great stories and songs of the Travelling community, some of which were recorded in the 1950s by the folklorist Hamish Henderson. The Stewarts spent much of their time on the road, Essie recalls, Travelling to Western Ross-shire in the spring before returning to Remarstaig, just outside Lairg, in the winters. And each year, when spring came back, they would venture out again along the same paths. From Lairg, Essie told Neat, 'our roads spread out all over the north'.

The pearl-fishers are sometimes seen in a nostalgic light, idealised as figures who maintained contact with the rhythms of the natural world when modernity was bringing most of us further indoors. As Neat makes clear in his book, however, the going could be very tough for people like Eddie and Essie. After their marriage, when Essie was seventeen and Eddie twenty-nine, the couple spent decades searching for mussels in the rivers of Ross-shire, Sutherland and Caithness, living off the proceeds of the pearls they sold to local jewellers. And although there were many joyous occasions – those mornings or afternoons when a clutch of pearls was found along a stretch of river – there was also the difficulty of the work, what

Eddie describes as 'the ache, the cold, the wet [and] the peeling feet' brought on by long days on the river. And, whenever the pearls were scarce, the couple had to make do with seasonal work on farms, where they were employed to dig ditches, harvest potatoes, grub out hedges, and whatever else was required of them. Eventually, the work would damage them both – 'Eddie's back went and so did mine,' Essie told Neat – and it is also possible that the strain of persistent manual labour, alongside the financial insecurity of life on the road, had a bearing on their relationship. In the mid-1980s, after being married for twenty-five years, the two parted ways for good.

During their time together, Eddie and Essie must have accumulated a knowledge of mussels and rivers unequalled in modern Scotland. And it was a knowledge that would have connected them to an ancient line of pearl-fishers stretching back to the time of the Venerable Bede, if not further. In his interview with Neat, for example, Eddie speaks of the different-coloured pearls he had encountered during his lifetime, from the grey pearls of the Spey, some of which carry a 'bluish tinge', to the 'rose-pink' or 'salmon pink' pearls of the Oykel, a river which also produces pearls that resemble the 'soft blue sheen of the ling' as well as the 'soft red glow of the bell-heather'. There were also the green, purple, and grey pearls of the River Conon, the 'satin-white' and 'silver-grey' pearls of the Laxford, and the milk chocolate and dark chocolate browns of other rivers in Sutherland and Caithness. And not only did the pearls have their 'different sheens', Eddie explained, they also had their distinctive forms. There were button-shaped and egg-shaped pearls, pearls that had rolled themselves into little barrels, as well as pearls that looked like buttons or that were perfectly round. And of all the pearls one could find, the round ones were most valued by the fishers, especially those that obtained a 'noble, pastel' lustre, since it was these that fetched the highest prices. Such pearls, Eddie told Neat, were the kind 'that make a life worth living'.

A clear ethic of respect animates Eddie's account of fishing. In his remarks to Neat, he explains how traditional pearl-fishers would leave whole colonies untouched, to ensure they did not overharvest from any one river. By contrast, the fishermen who started 'coming up in droves' after Bill Abernathy's famous discovery would 'work the river like a factory'. 'They slaughtered the Tay', and when they came up to the Spey, 'they slaughtered it' as well. 'It was greed,' Eddie continued, since it violated one of the core principles of the traditional pearl-fishers. 'We would know which shells to open,' he said, explaining how one could tell apart a 'crook' (a slightly deformed mussel which was more likely to contain a pearl) from a non-crook. But the newcomers 'would open every shell – wee shells, smooth shells – and that was that! They wiped the rivers clean.'

From Eddie's perspective, the catastrophic decline of mussels has its origins here, in the appearance of the new pearl-fishers. In truth, a slower kind of devastation had already been taking place. In the 1960s, many of Britain's waterways were in a state of poor health, damaged by decades of pollution and intensive farming. And the problems would only worsen in succeeding decades, as more of the country's rivers came under strain. The new fishers may have destroyed countless colonies during the frenzy that followed the discovery of Abernathy's pearl, and yet they did not so much initiate a process of decline as accelerate it. All this was also happening at a time when Scotland's Travelling community, or the *Ceardannan*, as they were once known in Gaelic, was beginning to vanish. In this way, two disappearances took place side by side: the loss of freshwater pearl mussels and the loss of the fishers who knew them best – a double extinction that marked the unravelling of a river-culture which had evolved over many centuries.

In one of his interviews, Eddie speaks of the 'subtle shades' that can be found in the pearls of Scotland's rivers – shades that are absent from the pearls of the 'sea oyster that supplies the big international market'. And as I read *The Summer Walkers*, it was this remark of Eddie's, among many others, that made me appreciate what is involved in extinction: not only the loss of a species, but the loss of a shared reality. The pearls from cultivated oysters may be more conventionally beautiful than those found in wild mussels. At the same time, they lacked what an experienced eye could see – that special sheen of a river-thrown pearl – a sheen that not only captured Eddie's attention, but which seems to have penetrated deep into his being, and indeed to have formed him in some way. When an animal vanishes, however, it not only takes its own particularities with it (the gift of its otherness), but also the space that emerges when two distinct forms of life meet. That space is nothing less than a shared world – in this case, the world of pearl-fishers and mussels – but sitting alongside it are the other distinctive worlds that arise through the process of encounter. Salmon have a particular relationship with mussels that is unique to them, which is different from the relationship between mussels and insects, which is different again from the world that forms between mussels and plants. We experience reality through each other, and because of each other, and the richness of life is also here, in that space of meeting and transformation. One of the consequences of extinction, however, is that there are fewer ways of being alive with others, fewer ways of sharing existence. The loss of one is therefore always a communal event, since it strikes at the interconnected whole of which it was once a part.

*   *   *

After our trip to Windermere, Holly and I maintained an irregular correspondence. When and as they emerged for her, she sent me poems inspired by our encounter with the mussels; and as I began writing about my experiences of Inverness and Windermere, I kept her updated too. Occasionally, I would also share some of the things I was finding online, and one afternoon, I came across an article that made me think of Louise and her 'Ark'. Not long after, I sent it to Holly, knowing she would be interested in it too.

Co-written by the freshwater biologist Peter Cosgrove and his colleagues, the article appeared in the *Journal of Conchology*, a specialist publication devoted to the study of molluscs. In the manner of scientific prose, it was written in a plain and undemonstrative style, and like most scientific papers, its title was reliably to the point: 'Population size, structure and distribution of an unexploited freshwater pearl mussel *Margaritifera margaritifera* (L.) population in Scotland.' For all the restraints imposed by these scientific conventions, however, the article was animated by an extraordinary disclosure: the discovery, in the summer of 2013, of thousands of freshwater pearl mussels in a little-known Scottish river.

A veteran freshwater conservationist, Cosgrove had seen large and healthy colonies before. He began specialising in pearl mussels in the 1990s, when he was a graduate student at the University of Aberdeen, and since then he has surveyed over 1,200 rivers in Scotland. In his thirty years of surveying, however, nothing prepared him for what he saw that summer day alongside five of his colleagues – a veritable metropolis of shells, with seemingly every niche of the riverbed covered in mussels.

It is never directly described, but the excitement of the discovery must have been intense. And after what one imagines must have been an hour or two of coming to terms with what he had found, Cosgrove's scientific training kicked in. For the rest of the day, he and his colleagues proceeded to survey the river as methodically as possible. They divided the river into three zones (upper, middle, lower) and further divided these zones into 50-metre transects. In total, 244 transects were marked out on the river, and for each of these the conservationists counted every single mussel they could see through their bathyscopes. (Some pools were too deep for human observers, however, which meant that parts of the river were left unsurveyed.)

The results were remarkable. In one transect alone, they found 4,200 mussels – and after they averaged out the population of all the transects, they extrapolated that the river was home to more than 600,000 of these creatures. The figure was unlike anything Cosgrove had seen before – and meant that, as far as pearl mussels were concerned, this river was one of the most important of its kind in Europe.

The colony that Cosgrove and his colleagues surveyed is somewhere in the northern reaches of Scotland. If you asked for the river's name, though, you would not get an answer. Given the perils mussels face in Britain and Europe, Cosgrove and his colleagues have decided not to identify the river, and in the *Journal of Conchology*, it simply goes under the title 'River X'. To this day, the colony's exact coordinates are only known to a handful of freshwater biologists, as well as the owners of the estate through which the river runs.

After learning about the existence of 'River X', I found myself constantly thinking about it, for the title seemed an apt name for many of Britain's rivers, although for different reasons. In Cosgrove's use of the letter, 'x' signalled the presence of a known treasure, one that needed to be kept a secret. For other rivers, though, 'x' is perhaps more fittingly the 'x' of a lost place, or even the 'x' of a grave. It is the 'x' of rivers that have become so polluted that they have lost their identity, and so the 'x' of ecosystems in limbo. But when I thought of Louise's project, it occurred to me that 'x' might also be the name of rivers that might come good again, given half the chance. In algebra, 'x' is the term for the thing one is trying to solve – and when I looked into its etymology, I learned that algebra came from the Arabic root 'jabr', which refers to the 'restoration' of 'anything which is missing, lost, out of place, or lacking'; a 'reunion of broken parts'.

The river that Cosgrove stepped into in the summer of 2013 is unlike most rivers in Britain. But there is no reason why, given the hard work of freshwater conservationists, and, much more fundamentally still, the rewilding of our relations with the living world, the lost 'River Xs' of the country could not be recovered, revived, resurrected. For that to happen, however, we need to become more generous neighbours than most of us are at present – kinder and more attentive to the other beings with whom we share the planet. Projects like Louise's were important, and yet they could only be a part of a holding operation. This is because arks can only ever contain so many animals, and because they also place the responsibilities of care and skilful stewardship on particular individuals, instead of circulating these responsibilities more widely within a culture. What was truly needed, Louise had said, was a profound transformation to our relationship with rivers – a transformation that would make breeding programmes and arks unnecessary. The future Louise was working towards was one in which conservationists like her would be redundant.

In the four poems she sent my way, all of Holly's characteristic qualities as a writer were at work: her humour, her exacting eye, her unconventional way of seeing. In one poem, describing the transparent mussels we saw under the microscope in Louise's lab, Holly compared them to 'out-of-hours / glaziers fitting a sheet of stained glass / with their muscular feet'. And in another poem, she describes the mussel as 'the river's old receiver', a kind of 'wet / handset' into which the river talks – and through which it hears an echo of itself. The same poem also celebrates the 'slow radiance' of a mussel's long life – all those winter lines, all those long summers – and describes the pearls contained inside their shells as tiny moons. Yes, that was it: the mussels as glaziers, fitting panels of brightness onto the river, and the mussels as telephone handsets, calling their neighbours, taking calls from them in return, and keeping up an ancient dialogue that has unfolded over hundreds of millions of years.

I liked and admired the poems Holly shared with me, and I tell her as much when we meet at a park in east Bristol. It is a place I have been to many times before, but which Holly evidently knows much better than me, for when we walk towards a Victorian-era boating lake, she takes me to the water's edge and points downwards.

'There are duck mussels here,' she says. 'Did you know that?'

'No,' I say, as we crouch down to look for them. 'I had no idea.'

CRICKET

We hear the gorse before we see it. Dozens of seed pods cracking in the sun, a dry snapping in summer heat. At first I think it's an electric fence, but then Liam points to some bushes and I begin to understand. The chatter was gorse; the heat was cracking open the land.

The end of July, on one of the hottest days of the year. I am on a coal tip in South Wales with my friend Rachel and the entomologist Liam Olds, and below us, about half a mile away, we can see the skeleton of the Cwm Coking Works: two towers surrounded by an assembly of gantries, coal bunkers, rusting pipes and conveyor belts. Thirty years ago, this is where thousands of tonnes of coal were lugged up from deep shafts and transformed into coke in industrial ovens. But then the mining stopped, the buildings were abandoned, and the valley began to reclaim what was there. On the day of our visit, we can see trees growing out of the coal bunkers, roots clutching concrete and steel, and weeds sprouting from smokestacks. Further off, on the ridge of the next valley, we can also see what has superseded this place: a row of wind turbines, the blades moving slowly on this day of little wind.

The gorse pods continue to split, tumbling small seeds into light: *crick, crick, crick.* But beneath the crackling is another sound, full of urgency and itching and need. When we ask Liam what it is, he listens for a while and then shakes his head. Then he opens an app on his phone, scrolls through images of grasshoppers and crickets, and plays some preloaded samples of their songs. 'Don't think it's a Common Green Grasshopper,' he says, listening to one of the clips. He plays another sample, the song of the Roesel's Bush-cricket, and then, as if in response, the same call rises up from the ground. Liam nods and gives us a thumbs up.

We kneel down and tilt our heads. The grass is dry and brittle, and as we push back the stalks they make the sound of rain sticks being gently turned, although perhaps rain sticks is not quite right, for the summer this year has been strange and unrelenting. The soil is chalky and dry, and for weeks the sun has been taking the sound of water away from the earth. On the radio a few weeks earlier, I had heard that a section of the River Stour, on the border of Essex and Suffolk, had simply evaporated, while the chalk streams of Southern England – the Darent, the Lea, the Wandle, the Ver – were running perilously low.

We flatten the grass, following the sound with our hands, and after some searching we find it: a small creature with brown folded wings, exaggerated legs and an impassive rigid mask. 'Roesel's,' Liam confirms, comparing the cricket with the image on his phone.

The creature tenses at our approach. It is tiny and pitiful and strangely put together. It is also very beautiful, with its delicate antennae and glossy eyes. We hover closer, to which it responds by shrinking further into itself, ungrowing by a few millimetres. Then, taking no chances, it jumps and is gone.

* * *

Liam was born in 1992, in a small village in South Wales. He was thirteen when his family moved to Coedely, just over two miles away, and he lives there still, in a terraced house facing the main road. The house was built in the early 1900s, when industrial mining in South Wales was in full spate.

Today, Coedely is a modest village, consisting of a post office, a community centre and some ninety houses. Not long ago, though, it was a centre of industry. In 1909, two mining shafts were sunk south of the village, and every day they plunged hundreds of miners deep into the underworld. A coking refinery appeared five decades later, with two cooling towers that would come to dominate the valley, and, as a new generation of men went underground, plumes of smoke and steam would have risen high above them. The mining continued for seventy years, until the pit was closed in 1986, and during that time it also never stopped: when some men finished their shifts late in the afternoon, others would take over and work through the night.

By the time Liam moved to Coedely in the mid-2000s, the collieries in his area had been closed for more than twenty years. Still, his life was shaped by the spirit of the mines, for this is where he spent many afternoons as a boy, looking for caterpillars and butterflies, and where, as a self-taught entomologist, he now spends most of his summers, surveying the insect populations of former colliery sites.

'It was just across the road from us,' he said during one of our meetings, describing the colliery in his village. 'There were all sorts there – men flying remote-control aeroplanes, kids on motorbikes, dog-walkers. For me, it was like a personal nature reserve, where I'd go exploring on my own and mess about after school. And at some point, I suppose I began noticing the wildlife there – dragonflies and butterflies, but also lizards and snakes and loads of other things I couldn't identify.'

When mining first came to this area, the changes it brought were fast and unrelenting. In the 1850s, only a few thousand people lived in this part of South Wales, the valleys being home to small communities of farmers. By 1900, the region had absorbed a hundred thousand new settlers, all drawn here for the collieries. Mile-long terraces sprouted along the steep-sided valleys, built from locally quarried stone, and in their wake came the miners' libraries, community centres and workingmen's institutes.

At the height of the mining, 620 collieries were in operation in South Wales, with the deepest shafts extending nearly a mile underground.

Just as quickly as the mines appeared, however, remaking the valleys from Llanelli to Blaenavon, they began to recede. When the coal industry started to decline in the 1920s, thousands of miners and their families began drifting away from South Wales, with one region, the Rhondda Valley, losing more than a third of its population in twenty years. The colossal event of industrial mining in Wales, an enterprise that deformed the ground, polluted rivers and contaminated the air, but which also forged one of the most powerful working-class communities in Britain, made up of proud, independent and fiercely loyal miners – this complicated historical experiment came to an end. One by one the collieries closed, the coke ovens cooled, and the adits, those narrow portals into the underworld, were capped with stone or concrete. And then time began to reclaim what had been left behind. Rain soaked through the coal bunkers, tree roots cracked open concrete, and dust gathered in the colliery control rooms, some of which, complete with working barometers, coal gas indicators and telephones, give the impression of having been abandoned mid-shift.

Afterwards, something remarkable happened. Grasses began to colonise the spoil tips, followed by wildflowers and birch trees, and as these plants appeared so too did the insects: moths, crickets, butterflies, ants, beetles, wasps. In turn, the insects provided food for spiders, lizards, shrews and birds, and as these animals appeared, more communities began flourishing on the spoils, including creatures that had never before been seen. In 2017, while surveying the Maerdy colliery, Liam's friend Christian Owen found a millipede that was new to science – a discovery that made the national papers and which is how I first learned about the collieries. It wasn't just the millipede, though. Since 2015, Liam has identified more than 900 invertebrate species on the spoils, a fifth of which are of 'conservation priority', meaning that they represent some of the rarest and most threatened species in Britain. Despite everything that had happened there, the collieries have become sites of incredible biodiversity, landscapes where life was knitting itself together again.

I wanted to find out more about the spoils and the insects that were thriving there. And I wanted to learn what, if anything, these places might tell us about the future. For at a time when it has 'become easier to imagine the end of the world than the end of capitalism', as Fredric Jameson has written, the collieries may help us out of this imaginative impasse, by offering us glimpses of a post-capitalist landscape: swallows nesting in a derelict factory; crickets singing among lumps of shale.

'When people think of South Wales,' Liam told me, 'they think unemployment, crime and all the other things that go with post-industrialisation. But what they don't see are the rich habitats the miners left behind and all the life on the spoils. And that's what makes these places so important. They're part of our heritage, but they are also what comes after it.'

This is also what makes Liam's story so interesting. As with his ancestors, he has stayed close to the mines – both his grandfather and great-grandfather were coal miners – but he works the land in a very different way now, noticing rather than extracting, and standing aside rather than digging down. He is a product of these places but is also something his grandfathers could never have foreseen: an entomologist of the coal spoils.

* * *

By now, Liam, Rachel and I have reached a hilltop, where we stand shin-high in wildflowers and silvery-blue grass. Swifts zipline overhead, careening along invisible wires, while the air in the distance is slightly warped, bent out of shape by rising ribbons of heat. Half an hour ago, we had met Liam on a road by the colliery, and he had immediately taken us here, where we would get a good view of the old coking works. It was then that we also heard the ground crackling, the sounds of crickets in the grass.

I knew that Rachel would be interested in the collieries. A friend from Bristol, she had been writing a book on insects in modern literature, and when I told her about the spoils, and the life that was now thriving there, we decided to write to Liam. Did he ever give tours of the coal tips, we asked, and might he be open to visitors?

'Come anytime,' he replied, a few days later. It was peak insect season, and he would be busy surveying dozens of collieries in South Wales, and yet he seemed pleased that strangers had taken an interest in his work.

From the crest of the hill Liam points at a vast structure crouching in the valley: a derelict mass of concrete and steel, with two towers rising from its centre. Between 1958 and 2002, millions of tonnes of coke were produced here, in massive furnaces that reached temperatures of 1,000 degrees Celsius or more. The coke was then freighted eastwards by train, to provide industry with a cheap source of fuel.

'I don't think it will survive for very long,' Liam tells us. 'Developers have had their eye on this place for years.'

Now that he has shown us the coking works, I expect Liam to lead us down the hill, so that we might begin our tour of the spoils. But as we follow him to another part of the slope, where he begins to name the flowers around us – bird's-foot-trefoil, kidney vetch, ragwort, pignut – it slowly dawns on me: the hill we are standing on, rich with plant-life and studded with shale, *is* the spoils. This landscape has been made by miners.

It is then that he describes the strange story of the spoils, one that continues to unfold in the most remarkable ways.

In their search for coal, Liam tells us, the miners extracted all kinds of things: mudstone, claystone, ironstone. But these were waste materials – rocks the miners had no use for. And so they were thrown out onto the land, in little heaps that gradually grew into massive mounds.

Over time, the spoils formed complex topographies of their own, characterised by varying gradients and aspects, and because the tips were composed of different materials, with different pH levels and soil structures, they provided the underlying substrate for distinctive landscapes to emerge. Bilberry-filled heaths formed alongside vetch-covered meadows, while patches of bare, free-draining ground surfaced next to scrubland. Elsewhere, grasslands sprang up beside marshy reed beds, which themselves appeared next to 'inland sand dunes' – habitats that look like the dunes of coasts or deserts, but which developed here under less natural conditions.

'Let's go down here,' Liam says, leading us across the slope. 'There's something I'd like to show you.'

We walk lengthways along the slope before scrambling down into a narrow gully. The temperature here is noticeably cooler than above, the ground soft and damp, and when we look down, we can see water gently welling up from the soil. The earth by the water is strangely discoloured, a mix of crumbling white chalk and dark patches of green and brown, and at Liam's invitation we poke the ground, which gives way easily and is cool to the touch.

The material is known as tufa, we soon learn. A soft sedimentary rock, it appears when calcium-enriched groundwater reaches the surface of the earth, sinters away, and then forms thick carbonate deposits on the ground, not unlike the limescale inside a kettle. And it's because of the tufa, Liam says, that all these mosses are here.

He points at the green and brown patches on the ground, and now, looking closer, I see that we are standing above a small wilderness. The dark stains are in fact mosses – whorled tufa moss, according to Liam – and as I run my hand over the tiny leaves, my fingers pick up the moistness they have gathered from deep underground.

The tufa is here because of limestone deposits, Liam tells us, and although the deposits may have formed naturally, there is every chance they were also dumped here by the miners. And because of the tufa, he continues, the spoils are home to a group of flies known as soldierflies, including nationally scarce species that require calcium-rich habitats.

It's a dizzying thought. Soldierflies live for a few weeks; the colliery – if it was responsible for the tufa – was in operation for nearly eighty years; and the limestone formed some 350 million years ago, from the shells of marine organisms that had sunk to the sea floor. And all these timescales are at work here, in a small gully in South Wales.

We walk towards the eastern side of the spoils, listening as Liam tells us about the plants we might see along the way: yellow flag iris, cotton-grass, southern marsh orchids, winter greens. These plants belong to very different habitats – grasslands, heathlands, wetlands, coastal sites – and in ordinary circumstances are usually found many miles apart. But because of the way the tips were formed, a hummock of limestone here, a mound of sandstone there, the most unlikely of plants and habitats have become bedfellows. The waste produced by industry is sometimes referred to as 'arisings', a word which, when I first came across it, I had mistakenly read as 'uprisings'. But as Liam explains the coal tips to us, the misreading suddenly feels appropriate: the spoils had become their own agents in the landscape, lively masses of self-willed matter.

We crest a hill, cross a stretch of bare ground, and clamber down a steep slope flecked with shale. At the bottom of the hill, a meadow gradually merges with a small birch woodland, and as we pick our way through the trees, we can see the beginnings of a reed bed up ahead. Coming closer, the extent of the reed bed becomes clear: what I thought was the edge of a small pond is in fact a vast swaying hinterland, with no end in sight. We have reached one of the largest reed beds in South Wales, Liam says, before telling us about the dozens of dragonfly species that we might find here. 'But you can also find Britain's largest leaf beetles at Cwm,' he adds, 'as well as rare species of bees and wasps. The variety here is just phenomenal.'

Since beginning his surveys, Liam has found hundreds of insect species on the coal tips, including thirteen species of dragonfly, twenty-eight species of butterfly, dozens of kinds of beetle, and one hundred species of bee. He has also found a variety of wasps, hoverflies, grasshoppers, crickets, moths and ants, and, among this heady mix, dozens of parasite species: specialist hoverflies that prey on a particular ant species, large flies that feed on beetles, and the dramatically named Ornate-tailed Digger Wasp.

Many of the creatures are commonly found in Britain, but others are endangered or fast declining, among them the Grayling butterfly and the Dingy Skipper. And yet here they were: the familiar and the rare, the abundant and the scarce; all sharing the variegated common land of the spoils.

For a few minutes, as Rachel and Liam walk ahead into another small woodland, I linger behind and look at the landscape we have crossed. In half a mile, Liam has shown us heath, meadow, scrubland, reed bed and woodland, and as I stand there in the sun, the oddness of this place strikes me again. Back in Bristol, I had read that the spoils contained large amounts of pyrite, which, after being exposed to rain and oxygen, would sometimes spontaneously ignite and smoulder on the tips for days. Occasionally, the fires were of such intensity that they fused different waste materials, thus producing a weird geological cake: a coagulation of the Carboniferous era, when coal was mostly formed, and the Anthropocene. Somehow, though, the insects have found a way of prospering in this strangest of places. Time and space may be out of joint here, yet the creatures go on.

I join Liam and Rachel by a stand of trees, and we find a place to sit down for our lunch. We remark again on the day's heat, talk about the things we have seen that day, and then Rachel asks Liam about his plans for the coming years. Does he have any funding to help with his surveys? And will the spoils be granted special protection one day, given their ecological value? To both these questions, Liam gives a rueful shake of the head. All his surveying work – eight years and counting – has so far been undertaken without any funding or institutional support. As for the future of the spoils, he tells us that they are always being threatened by developers, who seem to propose new 'improvement schemes' every year. Given what the spoils are up against, he says that simply preserving them would be a victory.

It can be hard going, though, being an advocate of these places. In any discussion of the spoils, a particular tragedy is never far from the mind: the collapse of a coal tip above the town of Aberfan in 1966, a catastrophe which led to the deaths of 144 people, most of them children. In the wake of the event, a nationwide reckoning of Britain's spoils followed, and in 1969 an act of parliament obliged local authorities to carry out 'remedial operations' on unstable tips within their jurisdiction. Effectively, though, what took place was the mass reclamation of most of the country's spoils, even those that posed no danger to nearby settlements, a process accelerated by the passage of the 1982 Derelict Land Grant, which encouraged councils to repurpose 'unsightly' landscapes that 'inhibit[ed] new economic activity'. From Northumberland and Yorkshire, to South Wales and Cornwall, more and more tips were slowly removed – a clean-up process that continues to this day.

Some of these reclamations were unnecessary, Liam says. Of the thousands of spoils earmarked for development, hundreds were in fact structurally sound, and so, as far as public safety was concerned, did not place surrounding communities at risk. More than that, their removal was ecologically harmful, since improvement schemes usually replaced complex habitats with simplified environments, usually in the form of industrial estates and new housing. Even spoils that escaped this fate were also harmed. To make them look greener, local authorities covered hundreds of spoils with fertilizer before seeding them with grass, and while the subsequent landscapes may have seemed more harmonious – more closely aligned with our notions of beauty – their greenness was also the mark of impoverishment, since they were no match for the biodiverse landscapes they had replaced. But most people don't see it in those terms, Liam continues. The tips are usually viewed as ugly or dangerous – usually both. In truth, they are the abundant places we did not know we were looking for, exhausted land that has somehow come good again.

We finish our lunch and head back towards the coking works. Liam leads us down a narrow path, into another stretch of woodland, and as we walk I pick up a few things that come our way: an empty bag of Space Raiders crisps, a twisted nail, the upper torso of a plastic X-Men figurine. Ten minutes later, we come across the rusted remains of a windowless car, its bonnet thick with moss, and then, a few hundred metres away, a pile of metal coils – perhaps taken from the same car – sitting on charred soil. We look down together, wondering at the person who must have come here one evening and placed these coils on a bonfire, and as we stand there, I see ourselves as if from the woodland canopy – three people contemplating a patch of burnt earth – and feel a sudden wave of vertigo. The coils are unmistakably of our time, objects from our fossil fuel age, yet they also seem completely antiquated, artefacts without any clear meaning or use. For a moment, it was like glimpsing the world that came *after* us, after our tenancy on earth had ended: a few human relics in a green wood, engulfed by life's rising tide.

We emerge from the woodland, continue up a steep path, and soon find ourselves near the hilltop where we first began, overlooking the Cwm Coking Works. Brown sparks fly from our feet, bits of living grass, and when we look down we see that we are surrounded by crickets. They are the same species we encountered earlier that morning, the Roesel's Bush-cricket, and there must be dozens of them, all singing the same dry song. Above, gulls circle in a cloudless sky, and across the valley we can see the towers of distant wind turbines, blades glinting in the distance.

Before we leave, I scoop up two lumps of coal from the ground. One I give to Rachel, and the other I keep on my desk as a paperweight. A few days later, parts of the UK recorded their highest-ever temperatures, and for many weeks after, whenever I look at the coal on my desk, I think of the strange things Liam had shown us: electric-blue damselflies flying through reed beds, mosses growing on tufa, and wildflower meadows interspersed with shale. For weeks, too, I could still hear the sounds that had risen up from the ground, the songs of crickets in the grass. It was the sound of mating and fighting, of need and procreation, an insistent drone that burrowed deep into my brain and would not leave me alone.

* * *

'How will you go about finding that thing the nature of which is totally unknown to you?' Meno asked Socrates, in what has become known as the 'paradox of inquiry'. It is also a question for our times. Amidst the messes we are leaving behind – exhausted soil, fragmented habitats, polluted oceans – there are also the weird flourishings happening at Cwm and other places like it. Since these revivals are so unusual, however, and so unlike anything we could have imagined, they have been difficult to see, let alone appreciate. Not far from Edinburgh, the enormous slag heaps generated by oil extraction between 1858 and 1962 have become important refuges for wildlife, and today these spoils – or 'bings', as they are locally known – are biologically much richer than most farmland in Britain. In Warwickshire, Bedfordshire and Sussex, former cement works now support populations of rare butterflies such as the Small Blue and the Grizzled Skipper, and in Canvey Wick, thirty miles east of London, thousands of plant species, as well as scores of endangered insects, have found shelter on the site of an abandoned oil refinery.

All these places are damaged zones, landscapes that have been profoundly wrecked by the logic of capitalist extraction. Yet some of them are now showing us what might emerge after decades and in some cases centuries of extraction. 'I was thinking the other day about the double meaning of the word spoils,' Rachel wrote in an email, not long after we visited the colliery. 'Spoils as goods, plunder, booty, and spoils as that which has been destroyed or ruined. Are the local wildlife now enjoying the spoils (i.e. the plunder) of what humans consider to be spoilt?'

Yes, that was exactly it: the goods that have emerged from plunder. No one knew that the collieries would one day host an unusual variety of insect species, just as no one knew that disused quarries, slag heaps and abandoned oil refineries would be so accommodating to wildlife. Inadvertently, though, they are now among the most successful rewilding experiments in British history, although they have never been known under that name. Unmowed, unfertilised, unmanaged, they have slipped free from our usual regimes of regulation and control; and because of this they have found their own way back to health, and in ways no one could ever have predicted. Damaged by our attentions, they have flourished because of our neglect, and now they offer a refuge for plants and insects struggling to survive in other parts of Britain.

There is no question that we need more and larger nature reserves, as well as more wildlife corridors to connect Britain's fragmented landscapes. We also need to farm differently, and to transform our relationship with landscapes where we have been overbearing. The resurgence of the spoils is inspiring, but they are only one part of a much larger reckoning that needs to take place, one that would take into account the totality of our relationships with the natural world.

Even so, the spoils might be part of that reckoning, for they remind us that healthy land might not always look pleasing, while apparently beautiful land might not always be healthy. The grouse moors of Scotland and Northern England are often celebrated for their beauty, for instance, but are in fact biologically denuded places, artificially maintained by a regime of cutting and burning. As for the great British farm, many of the UK's farmlands, for economic reasons beyond the control of most farmers, have become 'green deserts', drained of their ecological vitality. All too often, though, it is our chemically saturated, over-fertilised and all-too-managed land that is seen as worth preserving and fighting for, while species-rich brownfield sites are written off as 'wastelands' in need of development.

Not everything will heal again, at least not in our lifetimes. In countless places, human activity has left behind deep scars, and some of that damage – nuclear radiation, contaminated seas, the warming atmosphere – will haunt the world for generations to come. At the same time, we need different ways of thinking about damaged ground, not in order to feel better about the harm we have done there, or to uncritically celebrate nature's 'resilience', but because we need other ways of thinking about the future. In another letter about the coal spoils, Rachel told me about a book by the poet Denise Riley, who had written about the experience of losing her son, and who described that experience as a strange 'abundance in loss'. 'The context is very different,' Rachel had said, 'but I wonder if the idea of "abundance in loss" might provide a way of speaking about the nonhuman flourishing amid the death of human industry and community that characterises the coal spoils?'

It was a difficult phrase, but also a resonant one. We have lost an abundance of precious places and the losses are still mounting. Yet some of these losses have led to an accidental wildness, to a kind of abundance through loss. Of course, this knowledge should not excuse historical damage nor justify further extraction. Still, repaired places have much to teach us. They offer other ways of imagining nature's recovery, as well as better ways of imagining what our own healing might look like: not a return to some imagined, Edenic past, but greenery emerging from ruined ground. Today, some of Britain's forsaken landscapes are places where rare birds now shelter, without fear of their nests being turned up by the plough, and where reptiles, lovers of bare ground, can bask without interference. They are also where plant species of all kinds can put down deep roots, and where insects, both the rare and the common, are now plundering the land. In a million innovative ways, life can find a way of becoming abundant again in a damaged world. All we have to do is step back – the opposite of extraction.

* * *

Several months after our meeting with Liam, a strange tide swept across the world. It began in the city of Wuhan, at the confluence of the Han and Yangtze Rivers, then spread to the rest of China, and from there to South-East Asia and Europe, and then to all continents beyond. On the evening of 22 March 2020, the United Kingdom went into lockdown, and the next day everything fell silent: schools, streets, cafes, pubs. Residents could only leave their homes once a day, and for many that hour became an important reprieve, a chance to move in the open air and escape, if only for a moment, the grimness of the news.

It was during that time that I began going to Troopers Hill, a nature reserve in east Bristol. Twenty acres of grassland and exposed sandstone, it rises steeply above the River Avon, which bounds its southern slopes, and was just over a mile from where I live. I would often go alone, early in the mornings or in the evenings after work, although sometimes my partner would accompany me, and would always follow the same route into the hill: a dirt path that drops down into a narrow gully, skirts the southern side of the reserve, and then takes you back to the top of the hill via a patch of woodland. A green woodpecker could usually be heard at the bottom of the hill, yaffling away from its oak tree, and on a few occasions I flushed some roe deer from the scrub. Thinking myself alone, I would round a bend in the path, hear a sudden crashing, and then look up to see them bounding away, their still formal heads comically at odds with the blur of their legs.

At the top of the hill is an ancient chimney – a grey stump of weathered stone – and however you approach the reserve, it's the chimney you see first. Twenty feet high, it seems to watch as you come near, a sullen, domineering thing, and during my visits I would often see people drawn to it, touching the stone with their palms. Today, it leans at a slight angle, as though considering falling over, yet its lean will probably outlast us all. For more than two hundred years it's guarded its position on the hill, and before it falls it will see many more storms and frosts, convulsions and revolutions.

I liked being by the chimney. Like many old things, it seemed infused by a different quality of time, and during my visits I would also place my hands against its stony base. Standing there, I could see Bristol to the west, the Mendips far off to the south, and the line of trees that marks the presence of the Avon. And it was during one of these trips, as I leaned against the chimney, that I first heard them – the grasshoppers and crickets of Troopers Hill.

At first, I was conscious only of a crackling in the grass, a dry static at the edge of my hearing. When I came closer, though, I began to hear other things – clicks and chirps, pulses and rattles – and the more I listened, the more these crackles resolved themselves into distinctive calls. A fishing reel letting out its long line; two pebbles being clinked together, again and again; a languid maraca player whose bandmates had wandered away. *The grass is full of voices*, I remember thinking, and for many days afterwards I found myself coming back for these songs, drawn to the simple music of the hill.

After a few days of listening to the insects, I began to look for them. Some were easily discovered – you could flush them out of the grass with your feet – while others sang from deep within cover and fell silent whenever you came near. But soon I learned there was a knack to it. You needed to take off your shoes, so that your rustling did not alert them, and the first one I found in this manner was a cricket, which I later learned was a Dark Bush-cricket. It was strange to look at. Its legs were bent at a comical angle, its eyes did not move when I moved, and it was joined up like a set of gears, all whirring parts and intersecting levers. It chirped, fell silent, chirped, then fell silent again, and once it assumed I was a tree or a tall stem of grass, it chirped more regularly. Its dark-brown wings trembled as it sang. It clung tightly to a swaying stalk. It seemed too small for this big world.

Grasshoppers and crickets have equally distinctive calls, from the high-pitched fretting of the Great Green Bush-cricket to the dry rattle of the Meadow Grasshopper. But whereas grasshoppers begin and end their songs in the daytime, crickets continue singing into the evening, and as I spent more time on Troopers Hill, it was this night music that moved me the most. I would lie down in a small hollow, using my jumper as a pillow, and listen as the hill bloomed with sound: *crick, crick! crick, crick crick!*

What was I hearing on the hill? The joyful sounds of summer? The hopeful sounds of the earth? No, it was the

202

sound of pure need, for the lives of crickets are short and they have urgent work to do in the one summer of their lives: mates to find, burrows to dig, eggs to lay. And yet, even though their songs have no reference to us, I found that they offered a kind of companionship anyway. Their calls were little happenings in the field, small exclamations and earth-hymns, and sometimes, when I returned from the hill, I would find that the place had followed me home – in the grass that clung to my socks, or in the faint synaptic whirring in my brain, the sound of crickets in my ears as I lay in bed. Their songs were like the accumulated latencies of the earth, rising up from the soil, saying *I'm here, I'm here, I'm still here.*

*　*　*

Troopers Hill has never seemed so strange nor intriguing as it did then, during that year when travel was not possible and when I spent my time among the crickets of the reserve. And it only became more unusual when, during one of my trips, I stopped to read a sign I had never looked at before. It stood by a path near the chimney, and though the information it contained was sparse, it altered everything I thought I knew about the hill.

Long before meeting Liam, I had noticed certain plants on Troopers Hill – the ling and bell heather, the gorse and broom, the wildflowers on the hill's southern slope. I also knew, albeit in a half-conscious way, that these plants did not grow elsewhere in this part of Bristol, neither along the banks of the river to the south nor in any of the green spaces within walking distance. But it was only after seeing that sign, and after I began looking into the history of the reserve, that I understood why: this too was spoiled ground.

Long before it was a nature reserve, Troopers Hill was a place of work. Two hundred years ago, men quarried sandstone on the eastern side of the hill, while at the bottom of the hill they smelted copper. The copper was used to produce brass, which was beaten into pots and pans by Bristol's working class, and later some of these brass goods were traded for people who had been enslaved in West Africa. During the smelting, the sky above Troopers Hill would have been dark with smoke, the ground covered with ash.

And the reason the copper was produced here was because the coal was here. Three hundred million years ago, Troopers Hill was a tropical swamp filled with giant horsetails, tree ferns, club mosses and tall woody plants. Aeons later, after the swamps and plants had fossilised with time, humans began to sink pits into the ground and enter them with tallow candles fixed to their hats. Countless others followed over the decades, and the more the miners went down in search of coal, the more the city of Bristol grew up around them.

Over the years, then, Troopers Hill has been undermined, defaced, exhausted. Rubble has been dumped here, chemicals have contaminated the soil, and the face of the hill has been dug into and chipped away. Unwittingly, however, all this damage has led to a strange kind of beauty. Because of the quarrying and the mining and the smelting, the soil here has lost its original character; and because it has become acidic and thin, it supports an ecosystem that exists nowhere else in Bristol. Wildflowers thrive in the nutrient-poor soil, including heath bedstraw, sheep sorrel and mouse-ear hawkweed, and with the plants have come the creatures. A few years ago, an ecologist found more than 300 insect species here, an unusually high number for a small nature reserve.

'How will you go about finding that thing the nature of which is totally unknown to you?' Meno asked Socrates. That question had taken me to South Wales, so I could see for myself the wildness of the spoils. After reading that sign by the chimney, though, I realised that I needn't have gone so far. Like Cwm, Troopers Hill was damaged ground, and like Cwm, it had found its way back to health. The crickets here were singing on devastated land.

*   *   *

As June edged into July, more grasshoppers and crickets began appearing on the reserve. The grass was now louder than ever, and there were places where, simply by trailing my foot against the heather, I could thrill dozens of creatures from the ground. They leaped out in all directions, the small springs of a broken machine, and among these specimens were tiny beings no larger than a nail clipping. One afternoon, I caught one and felt it bouncing around between my palms. It was like holding a grain of rice that had come alive.

When I looked at it closely, I was amazed at what I saw. The insect was an exact replica of the larger grasshoppers and crickets I had seen on the hill, only it was many times smaller and had paler skin. And over the next week, as I searched for more of them, I realised that the Russian doll collection was more extensive than I had thought. There weren't just tiny creatures and larger ones, but a whole spectrum in between, as though some hidden assembly line were producing the same models of creature at different sizes. Later, I learned that these beings were known as 'nymphs' – the names given to baby grasshoppers and crickets – and that they go through several moults before they reach full maturity. With each moult, they fling their dead skin into the grass, in order to grow into a bigger version of themselves, and for a couple of hours after moulting, before their new exoskeleton has formed, they are especially vulnerable to the world. I don't know why, but I found that very moving: growth as abandonment, the creatures growing nakedly into life. *Last week is dead*, they seem to say, *begin again, again, again.*

That summer, I identified three species of cricket on Troopers Hill – the Dark Bush-cricket, the Roesel's Bush-cricket and the Long-winged Conehead – as well as two kinds of grasshopper: the Common Field Grasshopper and the Meadow Grasshopper. Though common across Britain, these species seem to be thriving here, where hundreds if not thousands have set up their homes. During the evenings, though, what I loved to hear most was the Dark Bush-cricket, which emitted a simple clear chirp. I would close my eyes, let their pulses fill my brain, and once, when I had been lying there for a long time, I was able to turn my head to see one moving in the grass. It froze when I came closer, then stayed still when I leaned over it. It was a large creature, about three inches long, and when it began crawling again, its movements seemed oddly formal, as though it were a courtier at a dance. It chirped, sending up its music from the grass, and not far away, by a patch of heather, I could hear the responses of another cricket.

From the articles and books I was reading at home, I learned that crickets began singing some 300 million years ago, when the rocks we now burn as coal were towering ferns, club mosses and horsetail plants. Their songs would have been relatively basic at first. Covering one of the cricket's forewings are tiny ridges or bumps, and as this wing is rubbed against the other forewing, sometimes known as the 'harp', the air between the wings begins to resonate. Because early cricket wings only had a few bumps, however, the insect's first stridulations would have been fairly simple, and it was only later, as the wing structures became more complicated, that their songs grew in distinction and variety. Today, there are some two thousand species of cricket around the planet, all singing the particular songs of themselves.

Crickets hear each other through another ingenious mechanism – a tiny hearing organ located on their front legs. When the air around them vibrates, the tympana or 'ears' in their legs do too, and this process, which sets their nerves jangling, alerts them to where sounds are coming from and tells them whether those sounds are made by members of the same species. This listening is aided by another evolutionary trick. When a cricket sings, either to attract a mate or to warn off competitors, a mechanism in its body is able to 'mute' the reception of its own sound. This mechanism not only protects the cricket's hearing organs, which would otherwise be deafened by the power of its own stridulations, but allows the creature to better discern other voices. I liked that. Crickets hear the world even as they sing into it, shaking sound from their wings while listening carefully with their legs.

The more I learned about crickets, the more Troopers Hill seemed to expand for me. And yet, in a pattern that had become depressingly familiar, the pleasure of discovery became twinned with the growing knowledge of loss, for it was not long after reading about the natural history of Orthoptera – the insect order to which crickets and grasshoppers belonged – that I learned about the severe decline in many of their populations. For the last hundred years, but especially since the 1950s, crickets have not fared well in Britain, with two species – the Field Cricket and the Mole Cricket – now close to extinction. The Wart-Biter Bush-cricket, once common in Southern England, can now only be found in a handful of locations, while the Scaly Cricket is also at risk of vanishing. It is true that, bucking these declines, some of Britain's eighteen cricket species seem to be thriving, among them the Roesel's Bush-cricket and the Speckled Bush-cricket. Other species – the Wood Cricket and the Cepero's Groundhopper – have also remained relatively stable. For most cricket species, however, as well as their grasshopper cousins, the story is one of decline, with a recent report placing nearly half of the country's species in the following categories: 'near threatened', 'vulnerable', 'endangered' and 'critically endangered'.

'A culture is no better than its woods,' W. H. Auden once wrote, reflecting on the close relationship between the health of a society and the health of its landscapes. To this, we might add that a culture is no better than its grass-music, since the presence of crickets, or indeed their absence, says something about our broader relationship with the land. Quick to vanish when environmental changes make their world inhospitable, crickets are also quick to flourish in the right conditions, and because of this sensitivity, they are known by ecologists as important 'bioindicators'. They are also an essential part of the food chain, especially for spiders and birds, which means that simply paying attention to how many you can hear can help you gauge the health of an ecosystem. They are singing for their own reasons, out of the urgency of their fleeting lives, and yet their songs are also a measure of a landscape's richness, and so, indirectly, a reflection of how well or poorly we are treating the land.

As crickets continue to disappear, two great transformations take place: the unmaking of the biotic communities
of which crickets are a crucial part, and – since nature and
culture cannot be separated – the loss of something deeply
human too. For animals are world-making beings, not only
present *in* places but part of the presence *of* places, and
since we share our landscapes with them, we also share a
common reality. What I was learning about crickets thus
confirmed something that I had recognised with eels and
moths, and which became clearer still during my time
looking for mussels in Scotland: when something in the
wild disappears, something wild departs from us too.

* * *

Crickets are strange. Their lives unfold according to biological rhythms that are beyond our comprehension and they
know things about the world that we will never understand.
They are aliens living nearby, strangers with whom we
will never become truly intimate. For as long as we have
co-inhabited these islands with them, however, their lives
have been closely linked with ours, and ours with theirs.
To hear them is to hear something completely beyond
ourselves – and to remember that the land speaks in more-
than-human tongues. At the same time, it is to hear an
aspect of our own story, albeit told in a voice beyond our
own. That story is filled with surprising variations, as I had
discovered at Cwm and Troopers Hill. But it is also a much

more ancient story than I had imagined, one that began 12,000 years ago, when crickets first arrived in Britain.

At the end of the last ice age, grasslands and marshes stretched across the islands of this archipelago, the first colonisers of the bare ground left behind by retreating ice. For the grasshoppers and crickets who entered Britain via the ancient land bridge of Doggerland, these habitats were perfect. Although some species in the UK thrive in dense woodlands, most prefer mixed open habitats – landscapes where bare earth and sparse grassland co-exist with tall grass and thick scrub. For Orthoptera, post-glacial Britain was a kind of paradise.

As the climate warmed, many of these habitats retreated, as grasslands and marshes gave way to pioneer tree species. Birch, aspen and willow came first, followed by pine and hazel, then oak, alder and lime, and as these trees established themselves, grasslands were forced back towards the coasts or into mountain glades. By 10,000 BCE, much of Britain was covered in woodland, although some ecologists now argue that ancient forests were much more open than previously thought, thanks to the effects of wind, flood and fire as well as the landscape-transforming work of boar, bison, elk and deer.

At this time, crickets and grasshoppers were not the ubiquitous species they are today. Instead, they were marginal creatures, found mostly on coasts and sand dunes, riverbanks and woodland edges, as well as whatever grass-lands and marshes had survived the expansion of woodland.

Around 3,000 BCE, though, a technology appeared that fundamentally altered their distribution: the stone axe. Across Britain, Neolithic people began carving out spaces in the woods, small niches that grew into ever larger clearances and which eventually became the sites of settlements and farms. By 500 BCE, half of Britain's wildwoods are thought to have disappeared.

For Orthoptera, these clearances effectively acted as a second postglacial period. Where wildwoods were cut down, grasslands and heathlands appeared, and wherever these habitats emerged, grasshoppers and crickets were sure to follow. They also flourished in other human-fashioned landscapes – fields and pastures, heaths and hedges, seawalls and ditches, spoils and rubbish dumps. And their story goes on in the most surprising ways. Once confined to the Thames Estuary, the Roesel's Bush-cricket can now be found on the coast of South Wales, and their spread is partly due, ecologists think, to the presence of roadside verges and flood defences – landscape features that appear to aid the insect's dispersal.

The first Orthoptera to colonise Britain are still widely distributed today, among them the Common Green Grasshopper, the Speckled Bush-cricket and the Oak Bush-cricket. They would have travelled from mainland Europe very slowly, advancing as little as 300 metres a year, and were later joined by the Mottled Grasshopper and the Mole Cricket. Once established in eastern England and Scotland, these species eventually spread to the Midlands, then to the western fringes of Britain, before finally reaching the Isle of Man and Ireland via an ancient land bridge. Later, however, when this bridge was drowned, more recent arrivals could go no further than the west of Britain, a process which explains why the Meadow Grasshopper can be found in Argyll, Cumbria and Pembrokeshire, for instance, but not in Ireland. In the intervening years, more species continued crossing from Europe to England and Scotland, until rising sea levels turned Britain into an island. When Doggerland was reclaimed by sea some 8,000 years ago, the route into Britain was finally shut. The great migration was over.

Today the UK hosts eighteen species of cricket, the living representatives of those ancient migrations, and every year these insects announce the return and passing of the seasons. When the grass remembers its music again, we know that summer has come, and when the ground falls silent late in the autumn, we know that winter is nearly here. As with so many other wild sounds, however, their songs are now diminishing in intensity, both in Britain and globally. For millennia, crickets have found a way of flourishing alongside us, and sometimes *because* of us, but now the forces arrayed against them – industrial agriculture, climate change and the fragmentation of their habitats – are becoming too great. A 2017 study found that a quarter of Europe's crickets and grasshoppers were at risk of extinction, while a 2019 report estimated that nearly half of the world's Orthoptera are now experiencing declines. Today, it is still common to hear them singing in the landscape, but whereas previous generations may have heard hundreds of grasshoppers and crickets in a small field, we may hear only a few dozen, and whereas they may have heard several species at the same time, we are likely to hear only one or two – a much-reduced field-music.

*   *   *

I can see the chimney on Troopers Hill from an allotment I share with some friends. In the summer, only its tip is visible, the rest being obscured by greenery, but when the leaves begin to fall in the autumn, it becomes prominent once more. To my mind, it is a kind of earth-dial, a reminder of the changing seasons, although sometimes, in more pensive moods, it also seems like a memento mori, one that sets me thinking about all the time that has gone and that is slipping away.

One afternoon, as I hoed on the allotment in late autumn light, I found myself reflecting on this book and the places it had taken me. In setting out, I had wanted to resist the lure of so-called 'charismatic' species in order to tell the stories of unloved and neglected creatures. But it was only when I looked back that I understood what had happened. Many of my journeys had taken me far from my local patch, in search of the vanishing and the rare, and yet, during all that time, as I went to the Highlands in search of mussels, or the Severn in search of elvers, the crickets of Troopers Hill had been singing their evening songs, animating their tussocks of grass. I had never really attended to them, though, had not let them in, and it was only during the Covid-19 pandemic, when none of us were able to stray far from our neighbourhoods, that I began paying attention to what had always been there. It was a kind of revelation – who knew the hill had so many voices? – but it also made me wonder: why had I not listened in this way before? I had tried to avoid one binary – the distinction between charismatic species and supposedly non-charismatic ones – only to overlook the wild things nearby. And yet what would it be like to listen to Troopers Hill for months, years, decades, so that one began to know the hill the way the chimney must know it? How deep could the listening go – and how much might one be changed by it?

'Everything has to be earthed,' an electrician said to me years ago, when she came over to inspect some faulty circuitry. And as I hoed that afternoon, her phrase suddenly came back to me. If we were to have any chance of getting out of this mess, then we had to fall in love with everything, or, if not 'love' everything, then at least pay careful attention to the common and the abundant as well as the rare and the threatened. We had to start earthing things again, and perhaps we needed to start with our bodies first, in our local places, with regard to the things around us.

Of course, simply paying attention will not be enough. If we are to develop a properly ecological civilisation, one that acknowledges the needs of the living world – and that incorporates those needs into our moral universe – then we will have to radically overhaul so many of our economic practices, as well as the political institutions that enable and support them. But even as we engage in whatever political mechanisms are available to us, while fashioning new political cultures through protest, activism and assembly, we also have to turn inwards, not out of a denial of the scale of the crisis, or the problems in other places, but because, in order to engage with those things, we have to be firmly planted in the world. And for that, all we need are our local places – a river, a woodland, a scrubby field – as well as our local neighbourhoods and institutions. From there, we might move outwards again, forging new connections, new alliances, and who knows where that might take us? In 1984, when thousands of miners went on strike in Britain, a remarkable act of solidarity occurred. A group of gay and lesbian activists in London began fundraising for striking miners in South Wales, raising over £22,000 for families in the Dulais Valley. That year, eleven other groups appeared under the title Lesbians and Gays Support the Miners, and began directing more funds to other mining communities in England and Scotland. And the camaraderie went both ways. In 1985, a Welsh chapter of the National Union of Mineworkers (NUM) joined the Lesbian and Gay Pride parade in London, the first non-LGBT organisation to do so, and later that year, at the Labour Party's conference, the vote of the NUM was crucial in passing Composite 26, a resolution which formalised the party's commitment to LGBT rights.

But where are the limits of solidarity, and how much further could we go? For the last few years, I had been thinking of eels as neighbours from the faraway, moths as bearers of earth-secrets and mussels as one of the gifts of life. They were all these things and more, and yet, under the aegis of capitalism, animals were also something else – part of an exploited and ignored underclass. In different ways, they are being damaged by the same economic system that has proved so harmful to human life, and if we are to truly care for them, then we need to stand not only *with* them, but *against* the processes that are decimating their lives. At one point in their classific-atory history, grasshoppers and crickets were known as *Orthoptera Saltatoria*, from the Latin word for leaping, and perhaps that is what we needed to do as well: to earth ourselves first, and then, once we were planted, to leap out in ever-widening circles of care and solidarity.

I continued hoeing, working over the last corners of the allotment, and as I did so I thought back to Cwm and the insects Liam had been finding there. After that visit, I had felt some measure of hope, something that had been in short supply for me in recent years, especially after learning about mussels and the slow death of Britain's rivers. For the colliery was proof that, even in the most damaged places, the world can remember its richness again, can summon wildness back onto the land. At the same time, I also thought of what had happened a few days after our meeting with Liam. It was the heatwave of 2019, one that broke records across the country and that caused train cancellations in England and Wales, out of concern that the sun would expand and buckle railway lines. *Given half the chance*, the spoils were saying, *life can flourish again.* Meanwhile, the heatwave was saying, *Things are only going to get worse.* These two voices speak at once, the wild and the terrifying, and although the second voice has become more insistent, that first voice is still there, too, full of its own vitality and strength.

What if the world's remaining wildness is asking something from us, asking us to become more generous versions of ourselves, so that we might learn a new kind of solidarity with our animal neighbours? Could we be earthed enough to listen, and then listen long enough to change?

* * *

I am walking to Troopers Hill late in the summer, following a route I have walked many times before: the alley with its resident jays, the path overgrown with hogweed, the narrow track by the allotments. At the main road, while waiting for traffic to subside, my attention is caught by a poster at a bus stop, which says: 'Bristol. Fast just got faster'. When I come closer, I see that it's an advertisement for fibre broadband.

I cross the road and enter the alleyway. Now that the day is over, I can feel my head lightening as it frees itself from emails and mini-emergencies at work. As I continue walking, though, my mind is snagged by a thought: can we go any faster than this? Is that what is really wanted? And now – I am at the end of the alleyway where the hogweed-path begins – a memory floats back of my grandmother in Yogyakarta, standing over the kettle in her kitchen. After the kettle boils, she will pour the water into a small basin, repeat the process three or four times, and in this way prepare our evening bath, and I remember being fascinated by this as a boy – the deliberateness of her movements and the slowness of time in her kitchen. 'Siap,' she would eventually say: 'ready'.

I reach the chimney on Troopers Hill and look out over the city. A solitary heron is winging itself home, flying east along the river, while a group of gulls circles above the quarry. I walk down the hill, into the small ravine where the heather is blooming, and when I look up again the edges of the gulls are outlined with light, as if they are moving through a golden liquid. They are catching the lateness of the sun on their backs, making it visible with their movements through air, and after observing them for a while I lie down on a bed of heather and close my eyes.

As I lie there my mind wanders, goes on walkabout. I think of friends I have not seen in a long time and of people close to me who are now dead, or I think of things I overheard on the bus or on the street, and as stray thoughts come in and out of my mind, I begin to do what I sometimes do when I am idle, which is to think up little letters to friends, oddball communications that I will never write, let alone send – *Do you remember, Leo, when you said that we*

are made of stardust and to stardust we will return? And Peter,
what should come first, peace or revolution? And as I think
about these things, the songs of Dark Bush-crickets emerge
from the ground of Troopers Hill, rising from the grass:

        *

                                                          *

               +

                            *

                            crick

                  crick

                                    crick!

                                    *

               +

                            *

     *

                                                        *

               +

                            *

                                  crick!

                  crick

                            crick!

                                        *

               +

                            *

Cricket

Dear Grandma, do you remember sitting on your porch in Yogyakarta, while moths fluttered around the lamps? The field beside your house was loud with cricket-song, and as we sat there you would search my hair for nits, while Dad drank Bintang beer and Mom sang the songs you taught her when she was little . . .

[Now the wind rises. More crickets join in.]

*

                                                              *

                +

                              *

crick crick!

                           crick!

                                       crick!

                            crick!
                            crick!
                            crick!

                    *

                +   *

Dear Michaela, if we are only here briefly, on what you call this 'marvellous unlikely orb', why aren't we kinder than we are, why not more full of love for this place? For context – I am listening to the crickets on Troopers Hill right now, which it would be nice to do together one day.

*

\+

*

crick!

crick

crick!

crick

*

\+

*

[It is getting late. The swifts are gone, the bats are arriving.]

\+

*

crick

crick

crick

crick!

*

*

Dear Dad, even though you are dead. On the radio this morning a scientist was speaking about the structure of water and said that, thanks to an 'angle' inside the composition of H_2O, water had a polarity to it. She then added

222

that, without this polarity, water molecules would not clump together, meaning there would be no life on earth. So, no angle = no dice, and for some reason this made me think of the earth's tilt in relation to the sun, which you said regulates the temperature of our planet and which is why we have seasons in the hemispheres. Which then made me think of something I read from Coleridge – forgive me, this is how my mind works these days – that Sir Thomas Browne had a 'brain with a twist'. Do you see where I am going? The angle, the twist, the tilt: life resides in these things. And now I am wondering: is this also what a species is – a twist on the tree of life?

PS, I often think of all the things you passed on to us, and all the things you kept us safe from – all of which have become clearer now with age . . .

*

+   *

crick

crick

crick

crick

crick

crick!

+

*

*   +

I stand up, shake the grass from my trousers, and turn for home. Bright bits of moon lie scattered among the puddles of the path and a handful of crickets are chirping along the allotment fence. I walk down the alleyway – the night has thickened, the streets have emptied out – and cross the main road, back past the advertisement for fibre broad-band. And then, just a few hundred metres away from where I live, among the tall grass bounding the local library, I hear it: a Dark Bush-cricket. The closest to home I have heard them all summer. I lean down and look for the creature in the grass, using my phone for light. Then I see it: brown wings vibrating in the dark, a cricket shaking the sound of itself into the air.

Thank you for singing, I want to say. *Thank you for singing in this dark time. It is good to hear from you. It is very good to hear from you.*

POCKETS
CAVES
FUTURES

On the afternoon of 18 December 1994, three cave explorers entered what became known as 'La Grotte Chauvet', or Chauvet Cave. Their names were Jean-Marie Chauvet, Eliette Brunel Deschamps and Christian Hillaire, and they were the first people to have stepped inside the cave, in southeastern France, for nearly 25,000 years.

As they explored the cave network, they soon found themselves in a new chamber, one so large that their lamps were unable to illuminate its further reaches. 'Our excitement grew,' they recalled, 'since caves this large were totally unknown' in this part of France. Advancing in single file, they then entered a narrower gallery, the rocks beneath them glittering with calcite.

Suddenly, as Eliette's gaze swept the wall, she gave a cry: in the beam of her lamp she had just made out two lines of red ochre, a few centimetres long. We joined her with beating hearts. On turning round, we immediately spotted the drawing of a little red mammoth on a rocky spur hanging down from the ceiling. We were overwhelmed. [. . .] Prehistoric people had been here before us.

As they continued exploring the chamber, they came across more images: the outline of a bear, a bird with outspread wings, a rhinoceros 'with an impressive curved horn'. It was not until later that evening, however, when they returned to the cave for the second time that day, that they discovered one of the most exciting parts of the cave system: a gallery containing aurochs, rhinoceroses, stag, ibex, bears and lions. They also came across a 'magnificent bison whose multiple legs evoked a running movement', as well as a panel of horses, each 'depicted with a remarkable realism and sense of detail'. '[W]e could hardly believe our eyes,' they wrote, describing the joy, amazement and 'minutes of indescribable madness' they felt before the horses. At the same time, their 'wonder was mingled with a kind of anxiety', borne of the feeling that they were 'desecrating a sanctuary that had remained hidden for thousands of years'. They left the cave towards midnight, exchanging the darkness of the chambers and their glittering rocks for the darkness of the night sky and its countless stars.

*   *   *

In 2002, the writer John Berger was given special permission to enter the Chauvet Cave. He descended into the chambers with a guide, equipped with a helmet, lamp and drawing pad, and after studying the various figures on the walls – two lions, a group of bears, the outline of a bison – his attention was caught by another animal: a male ibex. The drawing had 'a double energy' that was 'perfectly shared', Berger noted – the 'energy of the animal who has become present, and that of the man's arm and eye drawing it by torchlight'. 'Each line is as tense as a well-thrown rope.'

For Berger, the tautness of these lines was proof of a meeting. What he saw was not an animal that had merely been seen and then painted but a mystery that had been fully encountered. This is why the drawing was so mesmerising, and why cave paintings from around the world continue to seize our imaginations: when we look at them, we find ourselves in the presence of something miraculous, something that solicits our full-bodied attention while resisting our rational comprehension.

The rhinoceros of Lascaux, the bison of Altamira, the buffalo of Sulawesi – what might these painted animals say to us today? As they materialised on the walls of the caves, their flanks would have trembled in the flickering light, and perhaps, when the final lines were drawn, some may have seemed ready to step out into the world – a newly assembled astonishment. Look again. The raised head of that antelope. The bison's immovable presence. That faint scattering of horses, their forms glimpsed as though through a mist. Despite being drawn thousands of years ago, these paintings come to us fresh and unbroken, reminding us of a time when animals were seen as vital beings.

Today, the pulse that these cave paintings transmit is becoming weaker: 96 per cent of mammals on the planet are now livestock, while a mere 4 per cent are wild mammals. Increasingly, we are surrounded not by the strangeness of other souls but by the objectified bodies of agricultural commodities, and as more wildness disappears, the threads connecting us to the deep past begin to unravel. The 'double energy' preserved in the paintings grows fainter.

Even so, the threads are not completely frayed, for the simple reason that the cave paintings still command our attention. They whisper to us across an abyss, and as they do they set our imaginations echoing with feelings and emotions we still recognise. The paintings are a kind of samizdat, produced by a mysterious underground press, and what they communicate is an urgent message: that there is another way of being on the planet; a more generous, capacious and vibrant set of possibilities.

'They were for the dark,' Berger writes of the drawings. And they 'were hidden in the dark so that what they embodied would outlast everything visible, and promise, perhaps, survival'.

*   *   *

There are no historical precedents for today's ecological crisis. For the last 7,000 years, the environmental conditions out of which human civilisations have evolved have been fairly stable, and although there have been significant climatic changes before, and although prehistoric humans may have been responsible for scores of faunal extinctions, nothing in the past comes close to what we are experiencing now. Which is why things are so bewildering, and why the future seems so dark. We simply do not know what it is we are in, or what may be coming next.

In many places, though, communities are rising, resisting, organising. Pockets are forming – and these pockets are challenging the dominant stories of our time: extraction, consumerism, profit, growth. For the landscapes and animals that have been destroyed by these things, these pockets have appeared much too late, and yet there is no telling how much can still be saved by the work that is being done today, just as there is no way of knowing how much we are protected by the pocket-makers of yesterday, whose efforts may continue to support us in ways we cannot see. John Berger again: 'The pocket in question is a small pocket of resistance.' And such pockets can be found wherever 'two or more people come together in agreement'. These pockets shelter us, providing us with much-needed sustenance and courage. At the same time, they 'strengthen each of us in our conviction that what is happening in the world today is wrong'. They are havens from the world as well as places from which we might re-engage with that world.

*   *   *

For some reason, when I lie awake at night, it is the cave paintings I sometimes think of. There were children there – little boys and girls who accompanied adults as they worked on their paintings and who occasionally left their own marks.

In one book about cave art, I come across the following passage:

The footprints [found in caves] are quite often those of children: for example, in the cave of Aldène [. . .] or in Fontanet [. . .] where a child – who also left knee- and handprints – seems to have pursued a puppy or a fox into the cave's depths.

In another book, I learn that some of the cave images were left by children, perhaps with the help or supervision of an adult:

Of particular interest in this connection are the hand stencils of children, at least one of which in Gargas seems to have been made while the child's arm was being held by an adult.

I try to imagine what that must have been like. A few children deep in a cave, playing some game or chattering among themselves while uncles or aunts or parents worked on the walls. Later, a child goes up to one of the adults, curious about his goings-on, and places her hand on a nearby wall. 'Here,' the adult says, giving the child a hollow bone filled with ground pigment. 'Blow this across your hand.'

* * *

'Tell me the story again,' I say. 'I like to picture it in my mind.'

We are lying in the darkness of the room, talking late into the night.

'Well,' my partner says, 'it was my grandmother's first. She won it in a raffle in Denmark, sometime in the fifties. She then gave the Moses basket to a friend, who had had a child out of wedlock and later, when my mother was born, the basket came back to us. First Mum slept in it, then my uncles and aunt, and afterwards it was used for my brothers and me. My cousins also slept in it, Asger, Bjorn and Theis – and then my nephew and niece.'

We count all the newborns who have slept in the basket – Helen, Frederik, Aindreas, Josie, Jacob . . . Since the 1950s, the Moses basket has cradled more than twenty-five children.

'And where is it now?' I ask Catherine.

'In the corner of the guest room in Dublin, next to Mum's sewing machine.'

We reach for each other's hands in the dark. We know what the other is thinking now, know every turn of this conversation, its real and imagined terrors, its tender hopes.

Should we try? Yes, we say. No, we say. So it goes on.

The wildfires in the Arctic Circle; the vanishing animals of the world; the growing heat of our days. And not only the pitilessness of what is to come, but the pitilessness of what is already here. Famine. War. Borders. Walls.

Would it be right to bring a child into such a world?

Many of our friends have been asking this, and some have decided that no, it would not be right; for the next generation, life in the warming world that's coming would be a curse.

Still, the conversation continues – yes, we say, no, we say – and late one evening, while the house sleeps, I find myself reading Yeats's 'A Prayer for my Daughter', composed on a night when a 'great gloom' was in the poet's mind and a 'roof-levelling' storm was abroad in the night. As he paces his room, Yeats imagines the years to come – a precarious world 'Dancing to a frenzied drum' – and yet, in the darkness of that image, he still finds room for the most beautiful prayer: 'May she become a flourishing hidden tree / That all her thoughts may like the linnet be' and 'may she live like some green laurel / Rooted in one dear perpetual place.'

I go to bed that night thinking of that flourishing tree; the next morning, though, a thought flashes across my mind: but in a world without linnets?

The basket, I am told, has a sheen to its edges – the result of hundreds of hands touching the wood for more than seventy years. It has also been woven with great love, patience and skill, not a strand of willow out of place.

*   *   *

It is common to think of the cave paintings as a solely human endeavour, the product of the creative imagination, but perhaps this idea needs to be qualified or at least re-examined. The human mind summoned these creatures out of rock, making life appear on the blank walls. At the same time, the power of the conjuring imagination was itself bodied forth by the world of matter, drawn into existence through its encounters with and experiences of the living world. The animals were painted in freedom – the freedom one experiences during concentrated acts of creativity – but the painters, in their freedom, were also deferring to an external force, submitting themselves to what had stamped itself so powerfully onto their minds: bison seen in a valley, the passage of birds overhead, herds of mammoth moving, very slowly, across snow. The paintings are marks of wonder made by those marked by wonder.

The corollary of this idea is both simple and devastating: as more animals disappear from the world, they not only take their own singularities with them, as well as those intricate relationships they have formed with other species, but part of the meaning of the landscapes where they once lived. The earth becomes hollowed out, and since we too are part of that earth, that diminishing may also take place in us. With less wildness in our landscapes, we ourselves become less vulnerable to surprise, because we are less connected to a world of unpredictable flows and changes. Indeed, human wonder itself becomes endangered.

Of course, we should not care about extinction because of what it might do or mean to us. Rather, we should care about the lives of other animals because, as the American poet W. S. Merwin put it, 'Everything that does not need you is real', and because, as the Polish poet Zbigniew Herbert wrote, 'ignorance about those who are lost / undermines the reality of the world'. In these poems, neither Merwin nor Herbert was writing about extinction, and yet their words underscore one of the reasons we should care about the loss of wildlife. We should attend to the fate of our creaturely neighbours simply because we ought to care for reality.

* * *

I am walking across the saltmarsh of Severn Beach, on a morning when the tide is far out and the estuary is rippled by wind. Along the shore are flocks of redshank, thin legs bright against the mud, while dozens of Canada Geese huddle on the marsh, wings folded, heads turned towards the sea.

A few days ago, something happened that made us dizzy with possibility. It was a house in Ireland – or, rather, a series of photographs of a house in Ireland. The images had been sent to us by my partner's childhood friend from Dublin, who had recently moved to County Clare, and who, while exploring the local area, had come across an old cottage that was up for sale. 'Just needs some paint,' the friend joked in an email. 'But imagine – we could be neighbours!'

In truth, the house was falling apart. There were gaping holes in the roof, the walls were crumbling, and one side of the house had been colonised by ivy. But the house was cheap – cheaper than anything we could find in Bristol – and it also came with half an acre. 'Wouldn't it be nice?' Catherine asked. 'We could grow our own vegetables. Plant some apple trees. And you – you could finally have your writer's shed. Also, Mum would only be a couple of hours away, and if we ever decided to . . . well, it would make things much easier.'

'Well,' I said. 'Well . . .'

Later that evening, we spent a good hour looking at photographs of the house, discussing how we might fix things up. Then we found an online map of the area, zoomed in on local lanes and fields, and digitally roamed the landscape from our living room.

'And the sea is only twenty minutes away,' Catherine continued. 'We're always going on about how much we miss the sea.'

Flash of dunlin, call of curlew, and now the wind moving across the marsh of Severn Beach, visible as dark waves in the grass. Miles away, I can see rain advancing across the estuary, drifting like columns of smoke. The dunlin move up and down the shoreline, flowing like a strange kind of wind.

After looking at the pictures of the Irish house, we had gone for a walk to Troopers Hill, where we started to imagine – to really imagine, this time – what life in Ireland might be like. We had discussed the possibility before, but always with a sense of play and whimsy. Now, the discussion was a little more serious. Standing on the hill, we counted the years we had spent in England – many more than we had ever anticipated – and began to wonder: was it time?

I go down to the water's edge and watch the progress of the rain. After returning from Troopers Hill, I had felt the stirrings of adventure – a cottage in the country, new horizons, a vegetable bed! When I woke up this morning, though, I found myself pulled to Severn Beach, drawn to the estuary by some strong yet obscure tide. I wanted to see what birds were there, and what the light was doing, but I needed to work something else out too, something I could not explain the night before.

I begin skipping stones across the water, watching as some sink after a few bounces, while others, seemingly propelled by their own energy, ride far out towards the mudflats. My heart felt alive this morning, stretched open by a sense of possibility. At the same time, it felt tender and divided. The idea of moving to Ireland was exciting – and, with my partner's family being close by, it made practical sense. But even as I contemplated the idea, something in me had held back, and now, as I stand at the water's edge, I think I understand why: it wasn't fear, or at least not just fear, but something that might be called love. I was rooted here, in England. This place had become home – and not only for me, but for Catherine too. Still, I knew what she was feeling. Though she had her own strong communities and rich interests in Bristol, there would always be the pull of Ireland, the pull of that other home. Should we stay, we ask? Yes, we say. No, we say. So it goes on.

I continue skipping stones across the water, and as I do an old memory returns to me. I am twenty-one years old again, a few months into my stay in Bristol, and am standing here for the first time. I am a little dismayed by all the mud of the estuary, having expected to see a proper beach, but I am also excited by this place called England, by this world at my feet.

How much has changed since that first visit! When I first came to Severn Beach, I was a tourist. Today, this place is a part of me: the shape of the mudflats and the strength of the tides; the changing moods of light on the marsh and the different winds that arrive from the Atlantic. Now, I can walk this place in my mind, can recall every mile from Severn Beach to Aust.

As I continue making my way across the saltmarsh, I think of the elver that I had held during that night of fishing with Andy, some thirty miles upriver. Newly arrived from the Sargasso, it had been almost completely translucent, its body the length of a pencil, and as I recall that night on the Severn, other images from the last three years drift into my mind: a box full of moths in the Quantock Hills, the creatures at rest in morning light; a gleaming row of mussels in a Highland river, surrounded by trout and lamprey; and the crickets of Troopers Hill, singing in their tussocks of grass. When I began learning about these animals, I had no idea they would offer a kind of education of the heart. Over the years, though, that is what has happened. Attention to their lives has grown into something like respect, which has turned into something like care, and which, more recently, has modulated into something else. It is a feeling unlike anything I have known before, and which, as I walk across the marsh of Severn Beach, I can feel moving through me now: a tenderness at the great gift of life – the gift of being alive at this time and place – as well as a bewilderment at the rapid loss of our animal neighbours. And, alongside these things, a hopefulness that persists despite everything, a hope that keeps faith with the knowledge that transformations are still possible and that derives its energy from those small pockets of care and resistance that are everywhere forming.

The rhinoceros of Lascaux, the bison of Altamira, the buffalo of Sulawesi . . .

The lights flickering in the dark . . .

The miracle of what was – and what still is . . .

The sky in the distance has changed, has become dark with rain. I hesitate on the marsh, not sure whether to press on or turn for home.

* * *

Early February, the sky a chilly winter blue. It is a few weeks after that walk by Severn Beach and I am standing with a friend by the reed beds of Ham Wall. The reeds stretch out before us in a pale ruddy gold, and four miles away, rising out of flatness, we can see the Tor of Glastonbury.

'Not as spectacular as they used to be,' my friend had told me, describing the murmurations we would see here. 'But they're still pretty good. Fancy joining?' He had come here many years ago with his mother, who in turn had visited with her parents when she was a child.

We wait by the reeds, stamping the ground to keep ourselves warm. Along one side of the reed bed is a glassy pool whose surface captures and doubles the sky. The water is streaked with the white of trailing clouds and the yellow of the golden reeds.

Half an hour goes by. Nothing. Another half-hour. Still nothing. We scan the horizon, looking for the starlings, and as we do a shadow flits across my friend's face. He is worried, I realise, worried that the birds are not going to come. We continue to stamp the ground, two clouds of breath rising into the sky. The pool is now suffused with flushes of orange and pink, the beginnings of dusk light.

Then, all at once, an energy complicates the air. The people next to us begin to murmur and point at the sky, while others scan the horizon with binoculars and tele-scopes. Something is gathering at the edges of our vision, a series of dark moving clouds. It's the starlings – hundreds, no thousands of them – irrupting as though through a rent in the sky.

We watch them come – here they come! – twisting and re-twisting the helix of themselves, snowing their blackness across the land, now flowing towards us like some strange liquid, now flattening themselves into a long line, now expanding into the shape of a whale, and now compressing themselves into a hurtling disc, and as we look around us, we see that these self-making clouds are everywhere, all deep in the act of creation. They continue streaming towards us, splitting and healing the air, a thousand anim-ated peppercorns, a thousand shards of obsidian, and the patterns they make are so fluid and so unlikely that it is like being inside some hallucination, a dream-vision.

I glance at the pool beside the reed bed, the surface now a molten red, and when I look up again I notice how dark the horizon has become and how little light there is left. And now, as if heeding some signal, the birds begin to roost. The clouds begin sinking towards the earth, and as they do we can hear the *whoosh* of their bodies as they bed down on the reeds. We look across the marsh, where other clouds are also breaking apart, and for a moment the air is full of black rivers, dozens of cascades in the sky.

The last clouds descend, the pool darkens, and then – just like that – the birds are gone.

Acknowledgements

Deep and enduring thanks to Steven Lovatt, who listened, questioned, read, edited, argued and illuminated. Without him, this book would not exist. Thanks also to Peter Naumann, whose generous reading of the final manuscript (and late-night editorial phone calls) helped me across the line; to Anita Roy, who encouraged me to write in my own voice; and to Pippa Marland and Ralph Pite, for wise and sensitive comments on earlier drafts. Margaret Stead and Justine Taylor at Manilla Press were the best of editors – open-minded, exacting and endlessly supportive – and I owe a debt of gratitude to Kerri Sharp, whose attentive copy-edits greatly improved this book. And to Emma Finn, whose advocacy set this book in motion many years ago, my deepest thanks. More than a literary agent, Emma has been a scrupulous editor, a trustworthy guide and a tireless supporter, and I am grateful for all the care and energy she has poured into this project.

I am also thankful for the many people who I talked to for this book and whose stories have been critical to the shaping of individual chapters. Thank you to Andy Beddoes, Andrew Kerr and Emma Hutchins for their help with the eels; to David Brown and Chris Shortall for introducing me to the wonder of moths and the Light-Trap Network; to Iain Sime, Louise Lavictoire and Peter Cosgrove for sharing their expertise on the freshwater pearl mussel (and to Holly Corfield Carr for the gift of her poetry); and to Liam Olds and Rachel Murray for that unforgettable journey to Cwm all those years ago; I'm also indebted to Ted Benton and Tim Gardiner for their invaluable scholarship on Orthoptera, and to The Friends of Troopers Hill (especially Rob and Susan Acton-Campbell), for the wonderful work they do for the nature reserve. Many moons ago, I also shared the first chapter of this book with Gwilym Lawrence, and I'm grateful to him for his thoughtful edits.

While writing this book, I have been supported by friends, colleagues, networks and institutions, and it is a pleasure to record my many debts here. For humour, warmth, encouragement and wisdom, special thanks to the following: Andrew Blades, Nick Clough, Ben Cornish, Josie Gill, Julian Harrison, Stephen James, Sim Koole, Antony Lyons, Robert McKay, Adam O'Brien, Laurence Publicover, Michaela Rosová, Theo Savvas, John Sergeant, Jinho Shi, Jane Tarr, Judit Varga, Liz Watkins and Jack Young. Thanks also to Jessica J. Lee for early encouragement with writing, to the team at *Caught by the River* – Diva, Jeff and Andrew – and to fellow members of the School of Intuitive Herbalism for all those years of plant-led discovery: Polly Badham-Thornhill, Babs Behan, Amy Cox,

Acknowledgements

Nathaniel Hughes, Claire Loussouarn, Andrew Pegg, Annabel Pinker, Emily Thomas, Natasha Tillie, Heather White. The librarians at Bristol Central Library assisted with many queries over the years, my colleagues in the English department have been kind and generous, and The Leverhulme Trust supported early research into this book with an Early Career Fellowship. I have also been lucky to teach many gifted students at Bristol, who have taught me many things in return, and thanks are due to the Centre for Environmental Humanities at Bristol, which provided a forum for exploring some of the ideas in this book.

To Tila, Pablo, Melati and Kathleen, thank you for all your love. I hope you like this book and that it helps you understand why I've stayed away for so long. And to Helen, Fred, Aindreas, Lorraine and Charlotte, thank you for welcoming me into the family.

Finally, this book could not have been written without Catherine Gilmore, whose patience, strength and support has been the greatest of gifts, and whose love has lit up all roads for me. This book is dedicated to her and to our daughter Clara.

Notes

Epigraphs

Pages

vi *'Life is roomy yet, and the odds unbounded'*: Thomas Hardy, 'The Temporary the All' in *Thomas Hardy: The Complete Poems*, ed. James Gibson (Basingstoke: Palgrave, 2001), p. 8.

vi *'It gets late early out there'*: Yogi Berra, *The Yogi Book: I Didn't Say Everything I Said!* (New York: Workman Publishing Company, 2010), p. 85.

Chapter 1: Late Light

Pages

17 *'big wind . . . hurl and gliding'*: Gerard Manley Hopkins, 'The Windhover' in *The Major Works*, ed. Catherine Phillips (1877; Oxford: Oxford University Press, 1986), p. 132.

18 *'inscape'*: A straightforward definition of this term is not possible, not least because Hopkins uses it to mean different things in different contexts. Nevertheless, Robert Bernard Martin offers a useful summary of the term when he writes the following: 'When [Hopkins] said that what you look hard at seems to look hard at you, he was expressing his belief that when one understands a person, an object, or even an idea, through close study, that which is studied radiates back a meaning, one that is necessarily unique because each manifestation of the world is somehow different from any other, so that no two meanings can be precisely the same. Inscape is that meaning, the inner coherence of the individual, distinguishing it from any other example. It is perceived only through close examination or empathy, but it is not dependent upon being recognised; rather, it is inherent in everything in the world, even when we fail to notice it.' Robert Bernard Martin, *Gerard Manley Hopkins: A Very Private Life* (New York: G. P. Putnam's Sons, 1991), p. 205.

249

21   'nature-depleted': D. B. Hayhow et al., *State of Nature 2016*. The State of Nature partnership.

Chapter 2: Eel

Pages

34   'There are tides in the body': Virginia Woolf, *Mrs Dalloway*, ed. David Bradshaw (Oxford: Oxford University Press, 2009), p. 96.

39   'mud and moist earth': quoted by Richard Schweid in *Consider the Eel* (Chapel Hill: University of North Carolina Press, 2002), p. 72.

39   'Eels are bred of a particular dew': Izaak Walton, *The Compleat Angler*, ed. Marjorie Swann (Oxford: Oxford University Press, 2014), p. 122.

40   declined by 90 per cent. Adult eels have also been struggling: see D. Jacoby and M. Gollock, 'Anguilla anguilla', *The IUCN Red List of Threatened Species*, 2014, p. 7.

43   'The aim is to create ... a really hostile environment': James Kirkup and Robert Winnett, Theresa May interview, 'We're going to give illegal migrants a really hostile reception', *Telegraph*, 25 May 2012.

44   'Of course, nets are very different now': for a discussion of the history of elver-fishing on the River Severn, see Brian Waters, *Severn Tide* (London: J. M. Dent & Sons, 1947), especially pp. 5–8.

50   wrongfully detained, deported or otherwise targeted: see Amelia Gentleman, 'Windrush row: Javid's apology overshadowed by new removal figures', *Guardian*, 21 August 2018; also see Amelia Gentleman, *The Windrush Betrayal: Exposing the Hostile Environment* (London: Guardian Faber, 2019).

50   more than one million obstructions: See Barbara Belletti et al., 'More than one million barriers fragment Europe's rivers', *Nature*, vol. 588, December 2020, pp. 436–41.

51   miles of fencing ... to keep migrants and refugees out: see Angela Gennaro, 'La Ue non vuole finanziare i muri anti-migranti ma in Europa ci sono già 2 mila km di barriere: la mappa', *Open Online*, 25 October 2021: <https://www.open.online/2021/10/25/europa-mappa-muri-migranti/> I am grateful to David Suber for bringing this article to my attention and for translating it into English. See also Jennifer Rigby and James Crisp, 'Fortress Europe', *Telegraph*, 20 December 2021: <https://www.telegraph.co.uk/global-health/fortress-europe-borders-wall-fence-controls-eu-countries-migrants-crisis/>

51   'deport first and hear appeals later': Theresa May, House of Commons Hansard Debates, Index for 22 October 2013: Column 158.

52   'It made me feel like I was an alien': Michael Braithwaite quoted by Amelia Gentleman, 'Man living in UK for 56 years loses job over immigration papers', *Guardian*, 9 April 2018.

52 '*I felt like I didn't exist*': Paulette Wilson quoted by Amelia Gentleman, '"I can't eat or sleep": the woman threatened with deportation after 50 years in Britain', *Guardian*, 28 November 2017.

53 '*greater volume of elvers than of water*': Gavin Maxwell, *Ring of Bright Water* (London: Longmans, 1960), p. 52.

53 *once stoked huge fires along the riverbanks*: Tom Fort, *The Book of Eels* (London: Harper Collins, 2002), p. 188.

55 'poured *landscape*': Adam Nicolson, with photographs by Patrick Sutherland, *Wetland: Life in the Somerset Levels* (London: Michael Joseph, 1987), p. 10.

55 '*About a quarter of the British Isles . . . some kind of wetland*': Oliver Rackham, *The History of the Countryside* (London: J. M. Dent, 1986), p. 375.

55 '*fenways fearful*': this phrase comes from a translation of *Beowulf* by F. B. Gummere in *The Oldest English Epic: Beowulf, Finnsburg, Waldere, Deor, Widsith, and the German Hildebrand* (New York: The Macmillan Company, 1922), p. 83.

56 *continental Europe has lost two-thirds of its wetlands, while the figure for Britain is an astonishing 90 per cent*: the figures of continental Europe come from 'Wise Use and Conservation of Wetlands', *Commission of the European Communities*, 1995; the figures for the UK come from '2021 River Basin Management Plan', Environment Agency, October 2019.

56 *clawed back some 70,000 acres*: see Piet van Cruyningen, 'Dutch investors and the drainage of Hatfield Chase, 1626 to 1656', *The Agricultural History Review*, vol. 64, no. 1, June 2016, pp. 17–37 (p. 18).

59 *more than a tenth of all wetland species*: D. B. Hayhow et al., *State of Nature 2016*, The State of Nature partnership.

59 '*Thus have strangers prevailed to destroy our inheritance*': Richard Bridges quoted by Eric H. Ash in *The Draining of the Fens: Projectors, Popular Politics, and State Building in Early Modern England* (Baltimore: Johns Hopkins University Press, 2017), p. 158. In addition to Ash's valuable study, the following books have greatly enriched my understanding of Britain's historic wetlands: H. C. Darby, *The Changing Fenland* (Cambridge: Cambridge University Press, 1983); Susan Oosthuizen, *The Anglo-Saxon Fenland* (Oxford: Windgather Press, 2017); Francis Pryor, *The Fens: Discovering England's Ancient Depths* (London: Head of Zeus, 2019).

59 '*Our lands & inheritances are taken from us*': quoted by Eric H. Ash in *The Draining of the Fens*, p. 223.

60 *ancient fish remains in the mud*: see Claire Ingrem, 'Fish Bones', Prehistoric Coastal Communities: The Mesolithic in Western Britain (York: Council for British Archaeology Research Reports, 2007), p. 166–68.

61 *a man talking about 'Somewheres' and 'Anywheres'*: see David Goodhart, *The Road to Somewhere: The Populist Revolt and the Future of Politics* (London: Hurst & Company, 2017).

62 *possessed of an unusual 'homing ability'*: Friedrich-Wilhelm Tesch, *The Eel: Biology and Management of Anguillid Eels*, trans. Jennifer Greenwood (1973; London: Chapman and Hall, 1977), p. 219.

65 *'need for roots'*: Simone Weil, *The Need for Roots* (1952; New York: Harper and Row, 1971); see especially Parts II and III.

69 *'lost connectivity'*: for an example of how this term is used, see Steven Mattocks et al., 'Damming, Lost Connectivity, and the Historical Role of Anadromous Fish in Freshwater Ecosystem Dynamics', *BioScience*, vol. 67, no. 8, 2017, pp. 713–28.

69 *only 3 per cent of the UK*: F. Burns et al., *State of Nature 2013*, p. 47. The State of Nature partnership.

69 *1,000 hectares of the UK's wetlands disappeared*: D. B. Hayhow et al., *State of Nature 2016*, p. 10.

73 *the prevailing belief has been that the best rivers are quick ones*: for a defining account of how rivers and wetlands have been understood and managed in Britain, see Jeremy Purseglove, *Taming the Flood: Rivers, Wetlands and the Centuries-Old Battle Against Flooding* (London: William Collins, 2015).

75 *'nothing to do with anthropomorphism . . . us and other species'*: Richard Mabey, *Turning the Boat for Home: A life writing about nature* (London: Chatto & Windus, 2019), p. 240.

74 *'parochialism of humanity'*: Edward Thomas, *The South Country* (1909; London: J.M. Dent, 1932), p. 36.

Chapter 2: Moth

Pages

79–80 *Ravens were not they say . . . It was very dark*: quoted in *The Making of the American Essay*, ed. John D'Agata (Minneapolis: Graywolf Press, 2016), p. 7.

81 *'an example of a really old trope . . . a flood story, a creation story'*: Michael Silverblatt, 'Interview with John D'Agata', KCRW *Bookworm*, May 26, 2016.

82 *'reduced to about 150 souls'*: Pliny Earle Goddard, *Kato Texts* (Berkeley: University of California Press, 1909), vol. 5, no. 3, pp. 65–238 (p. 67).

83 *80 per cent of California's indigenous population was destroyed*: see Benjamin Madley, *An American Genocide: The United States and the California Indian Catastrophe, 1846-1873* (New Haven: Yale University Press, 2016), p. 10.

Notes

83 *as high as 30,000*: Felix Whitton, 'Conservationists are not making them-selves heard', *Guardian*, 18 June 2009.

87 *Common Quaker, Merveille du Jour, Flounced Chestnut*: for an authorit-ative field guide to Britain's moths, see Paul Waring and Martin Townsend with illustrations by Richard Lewington, *Field Guide to the Moths of Great Britain and Ireland: Third Edition* (London: Bloomsbury, 2018). Also see Bernard Skinner, *Colour Identification Guide to Moths of the British Isles* (London: Penguin, 1984) and, for a beautiful if outdated guide published in the early twentieth century, see Richard South, *The Moths of the British Isles* (London: Frederick Warne & Co, 1907).

91 *two-thirds of British moths have experienced sharp declines, while a fifth of once common species are now vulnerable or threatened*: Richard Fox et al., 'Moths' in *Silent Summer: The State of Wildlife in Britain and Ireland*, ed. Norman Maclean (Cambridge: Cambridge University Press, 2010), pp. 448–70 (p. 452). These statistics are drawn from Rothamsted's Light-Trap Network dataset and are based on records for 337 of Britain's common, larger moths.

91 *Netted Carpet, Figure of Eight . . . Least Minor, Sub-angled Wave*: see Richard Fox, Mark S. Parsons and Colin A. Harrower, 'A Review of the Status of the macro-moths of Great Britain', Butterfly Conservation report to Natural England, 2019.

94 *solidly English names*: for the fascinating history of these names, see Peter Marren, *Emperors, Admirals and Chimney Sweepers: The naming of butterflies and moths* (Toller Fratrum: Little Toller, 2019)

95 *may contain more than a million scales*: see Tada H, Mann S, Miaoulis I, Wong P, 'Effects of a butterfly scale microstructure on the iridescent color observed at different angles', *Optics Express*, vol 5. no. 4, August 1999, pp. 87–92 (p. 87).

95 *measuring some 100 x 50 micrometres*: see H. F. Nijhout, 'The colour patterns of butterflies and moths', *Scientific American*, vol. 245, no. 5, November 1981, pp. 140–53 (p. 140). However, it should be noted that there is considerable variation in the size of moth and butterfly scales: the scale lengths of some species can be 40 micrometres, for instance, while others can be 500 micrometres or more. For more detail, see Thomas J. Simonsen and Niels P. Kristensen, 'Scale length/wing length correlation in Lepidoptera (Insecta)', *Journal of Natural History*, vol. 37, issue 6, 2003, pp. 673–79. My thanks to Thomas Neil for bringing this article to my attention.

95 *The iridescence of a wing*: see Helen Ghiradella, 'Structure of Iridescent Lepidopteran Scales: Variations on Several Themes', *Annals of the Entomological Society of America*, vol. 77, issue 6, November 1984, pp. 637–45.

100   *designed by British entomologist C. B. Williams*: for his discussion of this trap, see C. B. Williams 'The Rothamsted light trap', *Proceedings of the Royal Entomological Society London*, vol. 23, issue 7–9, September 1948, pp. 80–85.

104   *total abundance of moths has decreased by 28 per cent . . . nearly 40 per cent of the country's species have lost half of their populations*: see R. Fox et al., *The State of Britain's Larger Moths 2013*, Butterfly Conservation and Rothamsted Research, Wareham, Dorset, UK. According to the most recent survey, published in 2021, total moth abundance has declined by 33 per, while 41 per cent of British moth species have experienced significant declines. (See R. Fox et al, *The State of Britain's Larger Moths 2021*, Butterfly Conservation, Rothamsted Research and UK Centre for Ecology & Hydrology, Wareham, Dorset, UK.)

105   *more than half of Britain's species are in decline, with some species losing as much as 98 or 99 per cent of their populations*: see R. Fox et al., *The State of Britain's Larger Moths 2013*. The 2021 survey provides updated figures: it shows a decrease for 41 per cent of Britain's moth species and an increase for 10 per cent.

105   *The numbers were hard to fathom*: these figures can be found in R. Harrington, 'The Rothamsted Insect Survey strikes gold', in *Antenna*, vol. 38, no. 3, 2014, pp. 158–66.

107–08   *'in this still place . . . They know Earth-secrets that know not I'*: Thomas Hardy, 'An August Midnight' in *Thomas Hardy: The Complete Poems*, p. 147. I am grateful to Ralph Pite for bringing this poem to my attention.

108   *'small kingdoms'*: Mary Oliver, 'Sleeping in the Forest' in *Twelve Moons* (Boston: Little, Brown and Company, 1979), p. 3.

108   *'I learned that the ground was alive . . . I moved in the great mystery'*: Tomas Tranströmer, *The Great Enigma: New Collected Poems*, trans. Robin Fulton (1987; New York: New Directions, 2006), p. 239.

108   *have evolved to absorb the echolocations of bats*: see Z. Shen et al., 'Biomechanics of a moth scale at ultrasonic frequencies', *The Proceedings of the National Academy of Science*, vol. 115, no. 48, November 2018, pp. 12200–2205.

108   *is able to discern the direction of the winds*: see Jason W. Chapman et. al., 'Wind Selection and Drift Compensation Optimize Migratory Pathways in a High-Flying Moth', *Current Biology*, vol. 18, issue 7, June 2008, pp. 514–18.

110   *'All of a sudden . . . the heavens had opened'*: Hugh Raffles, *Insectopedia* (New York: Vintage Books, 2011), p. 7; for a comprehensive account of insect flight, see C. G. Johnson, *Migration and Dispersal of Insects by Flight* (London: Methuen, 1969).

Notes

110–11   *'"Come quick!" . . . to keep up his courage'*: Jean Henri Fabre, *The Life of the Caterpillar*, trans. Alexander Teixeira de Mattos (London: Hodder and Stoughton, 1912), p. 248–50.

111   *'thickly bordered with lilac and rose trees . . . to reach the object of his pilgrimage'*: Ibid., p. 251.

112   *'certain rays'*: Ibid., p. 252.

112   *'delicate vibrations . . . extremely sensitive microphone'*: Ibid., p. 263.

112   *signals known as 'recognition pheromones'*: see Mark Young, *The Natural History of Moths* (London: T. & A. D. Poyser, 1997), pp. 150–68.

113   'I know nothing . . . blowing through the outer heavens': Antoine de Saint-Exupéry, *Wind, Sand and Stars*, trans. Lewis Galantière (1939; London: Heinemann, 1975), pp. 167–68.

116   *'one mighty alphabet'*: Samuel Taylor Coleridge, 'The Destiny of Nations: A Vision' in *The Complete Poetical Works of Samuel Taylor Coleridge: Including Poems and Versions of Poems now Published for the First Time*, ed. Ernest Hartley Coleridge, (1817; Oxford: Oxford University Press, 2015), vol. 1, p. 132.

117   *in place of 'symbols', read 'biosemiotics'*: for a comprehensive account of biosemiotics, see Jesper Hoffmeyer, *Biosemiotics: An Examination into the Signs of Life and the Life of Signs* (Chicago: University of Chicago Press, 2009).

118   *773 libraries were closed*: see Alison Flood, 'Britain has closed almost 800 libraries since 2010, figures show', *Guardian*, 6 December 2019.

119   *there are 14 million fewer books in England's public libraries*: Ben Riley Smith, '14 million fewer books available in libraries than when David Cameron took office', *Telegraph*, 16 January 2016.

120   *constitute nothing less than a 'lost decade'*: See Polly Toynbee and David Walker, *The Lost Decade: 2010–2020, and What Lies Ahead for Britain* (London: Guardian Faber, 2020).

120   *The Bordered Gothic, the Brighton Wainscot, the Orange Upperwing*: see R. Fox et al., *The State of Britain's Larger Moths 2013*. Butterfly Conservation and Rothamsted Research, Wareham, Dorset, UK, p. 1.

120   *Bedworth Heath, New Cross . . . Old Monkland, Eggbuckland, Tothill*: these names are taken from a much larger list compiled by Iain Anstice, author of *Public Library News: What's Happening to your Library?* See <https://www.publiclibrariesnews.com/users/old-lists-arranged-by-uk-library-service/news-topics>

125   *'It was the feline moth – the* Cerura erminea*'*: for his account of this discovery, see David Brown, 'The first British record of Feline *Cerura erminea* (Esper, 1783)', *Atropos*, issue 64, 2019, pp. 38–43.

Chapter 3: Mussel

Pages

131   *what he came across that day was a scene of devastation*: see Marek Vahula, 'Estonia's eldest freshwater pearl mussel', *Estonian Nature* (2013), no. 2, p. 59 (p. 59). My thanks to Õie Tähtla for translating this article from the original.

132   *place the cross-section in a glutaraldehyde solution*: Ibid.

132   *these rings contain many secrets*: as an example of what can be gleaned from these shells, see Joakim Nyström et al., 'Environmental History as Reflected by Freshwater Pearl Mussels in the River Vramsån, Southern Sweden' *Ambio*, vol. 25, no. 5, August 1996, pp. 350–55.

134   *'formerly called Albion . . . excellent pearls of all colours'*: Bede, *Ecclesiastical History of the English Nation*, trans. John Stevens, revised by L. C. Jane (London: J. M. Dent, 1954), pp. 4–5.

136   *a single creature can filter up to fifty litres of water a day*: Iain Sime, *River Runners: A tale of protected species* (Perth: Scottish Natural Heritage, 2003), p. 3.

138   *'shellfish may have been a critical food source' . . . modern humans found a coastal route 'out of Africa via the Red Sea coast'*: C. Marean et al., 'Early human use of marine resources and pigment in South Africa during the Middle Pleistocene' *Nature*, vol. 449, October 2007, pp. 905–08 (p. 907); also see R. C. Walter et al., 'Early human occupation of the Red Sea coast of Eritrea during the last interglacial', *Nature*, vol. 405, May 2000, pp. 65–69.

138   *'pigtoe and wartyback . . . Fluted Shells and Salina Muckets'*: for these and other names, see James D. Williams et al., 'A Revised List of the Freshwater Mussels (Mollusca: Bivalvia: Unionida) of the United States and Canada', *Freshwater Mollusk Biology and Conservation*, vol. 20, no. 2, October 2017, pp. 33–58.

139   *the population has sunk by 95 per cent*: see E. Degerman et al., 'Restoration of Freshwater Pearl Mussel Streams', WWF Sweden, Solna, 2009, p. 5.

141   In 2020, Scottish Natural Heritage renamed itself NatureScot.

155   *'gift goes around a corner'*: Lewis Hyde, *The Gift: Imagination and the Erotic Life of Property* (1979; London: Vintage, 1999), p. 16.

156   *'The only essential is this . . . the gift must always move'*: Ibid., p. 4.

160   *the Environment Agency has lost nearly two-thirds of its budget*: see Sandra Laville, 'Cutbacks stopping vital work on river pollution and floods in England', *Guardian*, 22 June 2021.

160   *Natural England has lost half its funding and shed a thousand environmental inspectors*: see Polly Toynbee and David Walker, 'The lost decade: the hidden story of how austerity broke Britain', *Guardian*, 3 March 2020.

167   *'living a traditional semi-nomadic lifestyle . . . their lives on the road'*: Timothy Neat, *The Summer Walkers: Travelling People and Pearl-Fishers in the Highlands of Scotland* (1996; Edinburgh: Birlinn, 2016), p. vii.

169   *'our roads spread out all over the north'*: Ibid., p. 5.

170   *'the ache, the cold, the wet [and] the peeling feet'*: Ibid., p. 114.

170   *'Eddie's back went and so did mine'*: Ibid., p. 132.

170–71 *'bluish tinge . . . make a life worth living'*: Ibid., p. 116.

171   *'coming up in droves . . . work the river like a factory'*: Ibid., p. 108.

171   *'We would know which shells to open . . . They wiped the rivers clean'*: Ibid., p. 114.

172   *in a state of poor health*: see Nigel Holmes and Paul Raven, *Rivers* (London: Bloomsbury Wildlife, 2014), especially pp. 51–54.

172   *'subtle shades . . . sea oyster that supplies the big international market'*: Neat, *The Summer Walkers*, p. 117.

174   *the article appeared in the Journal of Conchology*: see Peter Cosgrove et al., 'Population size, structure and distribution of an unexploited freshwater pearl mussel *Margaritifera margaritifera* (l.) population in Scotland', *Journal of Conchology*, vol. 41, no. 5, October 2014, pp. 541–52.

177   *'out-of-hours . . . with their muscular feet'*: Holly Corfield Carr, 'The Scale', unpublished poem, 2019.

177   *'the river's old receiver . . . slow radiance'*: Holly Corfield Carr, 'a man, an animal, a lamina', *Poetry London*, Issue 97, 2020.

Chapter 4: Cricket

Pages

184   *only a few thousand people lived in this part of South Wales*: for population figures, I have drawn on information compiled by Coalfield Web Materials: <http://www.agor.org.uk/cwm/themes/life/society/migration.asp>

185   *620 collieries were in operation*: this figure is cited by Stephen Hughes et al., in *Collieries of Wales: Engineering and Architecture* (New Inn: Royal Commission on the Ancient and Historical Monuments of Wales, 1994), p. 10.

185   *began drifting away from South Wales*: <http://www.agor.org.uk/cwm/themes/life/economy/>

186   *'easier to imagine the end of the world than the end of capitalism'*: Fredric Jameson, 'Future City', *New Left Review* 21 (May–June 2003), p. 76. Although Jameson prefaces this quote by saying 'Someone once said', it appears that he is recalling one of his own formulations: 'It seems to be easier for us today to imagine the thoroughgoing deterioration of the earth and of nature than the breakdown of late capitalism'. *The Seeds of Time* (New York: Columbia University Press, 1994), p. xii.

189　*complex topographies of their own*: for a more detailed description, see Liam Olds and Richard Wistow, 'Colliery-spoil biodiversity of the South Wales Valleys', *British Wildlife*, vol. 30, no. 2, December 2018, pp. 108–115.

191　*a variety of wasps, hoverflies, grasshoppers*: for an overview of some of the species found on the spoils, see Liam Olds, 'Invertebrate conservation value of colliery spoil habitats in South Wales', September 2019: <http://www.collieryspoil.com/_files/ugd/dccabd_bb278c9d-887f433fb0af9e6dd285df8e.pdf≥

193　*in 1969 an act of parliament*: the legislation, known as the Mines and Quarries (Tips) Act, can be accessed here: https://www.legislation.gov.uk/ukpga/1969/10/enacted>

193　*'unsightly' landscapes that 'inhibit[ed] new economic activity'*: see National Audit Office, *The Department of the Environment Derelict Land Grant* (London: HMSO, 1988), p. 1.

196　*'How will you go about finding that thing the nature of which is totally unknown to you?'*: this quote appears in Rebecca Solnit's *A Field Guide to Getting Lost* (Edinburgh: Canongate, 2006), p. 4. The line – and the larger passage of which it is a part – has also been translated as follows: 'And how will you search for something, Socrates, if you don't know at all what it is? What sort of thing from among those you don't know will you make the target of your search?' Plato, *Meno and Phaedo*, ed. David Sedley, trans. Alex Long (Cambridge: Cambridge University Press, 2010), p. 14.

196　*the enormous slag heaps generated by oil extraction*: see Cal Flynn, *Islands of Abandonment: Life in the Post-Human Landscape* (London: William Collins, 2021), pp. 15–40.

196　*support populations of rare butterflies:* some examples are Bishop's Hill (Warwickshire), Sundon Quarry (Bedfordshire), and Beeding Quarry (Sussex).

197　*Canvey Wick . . . shelter on the site of an abandoned oil refinery*: see Patrick Barkham, 'Canvey Wick: the Essex 'rainforest' that is home to Britain's rarest insects', *Guardian*, 15 October 2017.

199　*'abundance in loss'*: Denise Riley, *Time Lived, Without its Flow* (London: Picador, 2012), p. 84.

205　*an ecologist found more than 300 insect species here*: David J. Gibbs, 'Invertebrate Monitoring of Troopers Hill, Bristol', Report to Friends of Troopers Hill, 2019.

207　*began singing some 300 million years ago*: see Daniel Otte, 'Evolution of Cricket Songs', *Journal of Orthoptera Research*, no. 1, December 1992, pp. 25–49; see also John Himmelman, *Cricket Radio: Tuning in the Night-Singing Insects* (Harvard: Harvard University Press, 2011).

Notes

208 *When the air around them vibrates*: see Ted Benton, *Grasshoppers and Crickets* (London: Collins, 2012), pp. 54–58.

208 *'mute' the reception of its own sound*: See Peter Simmons and David Young, *Nerve Cells and Animal Behaviour* (Cambridge: Cambridge University Press, 2010), p. 223; also see J. F. A. Poulet, 'Corollary discharge inhibition and audition in the stridulating cricket', *Journal of Comparative Physiology*, vol. 191, October 2005, pp. 979–86.

209 *the following categories . . . 'near threatened', 'vulnerable', 'endangered' and 'critically endangered'*: Peter Sutton, 'A review of the Orthoptera (grasshoppers and crickets) and allied species of Great Britain. Orthoptera, Dictyoptera, Dermaptera, Phasmida', Species Status No. 21, Natural England Commissioned Report NECR 187, 2015.

209 *'A culture is no better than its woods'*: W. H. Auden, 'Bucolics' in *The Shield of Achilles* (London: Faber and Faber, 1955), p. 19.

209 *they are known by ecologists as important 'bioindicators'*: for example, see Corinna S. Bazelet and Michael J. Samways, 'Identifying grasshopper bioindicators for habitat quality assessment of ecological networks', *Ecological Indicators*, vol. 11, September 2011, pp. 1259–269.

212 *not the ubiquitous species they are today:* see D. R. Ragge, *Grasshoppers, Crickets and Cockroaches of the British Isles* (London: Frederick Warne & Co, 1965), pp. 269–70. For a comprehensive and up-to-date guide to British Orthoptera, see Ted Benton, *Grasshoppers & Crickets* (London: Collins, 2012).

212 *grasslands and heathlands appeared*: see D. R. Ragge, *Grasshoppers, Crickets and Cockroaches of the British Isles*, p. 269.

212 *appear to aid the insect's dispersal*: see Ted Benton, *Grasshoppers & Crickets*, p. 459; for a Swedish study of how 'linear landscape elements' might aid dispersal of the Roesel's bush-cricket, see Å. Berggren, A. Carlson, and O. Kindvall 'The effect of landscape composition on colonization success, growth rate and dispersal in introduced bush-crickets *Metrioptera roeseli'*, *Journal of Animal Ecology*, vol. 70, issue 4, December 2001, pp. 663–70.

213 *advancing as little as 300 metres a year:* see Godfrey M. Hewitt, 'Post-glacial re-colonization of European biota', *Biological Journal of the Linnean Society*, vol. 68, issue 1–2, September 1999, pp. 87–112 (p. 91).

213 *could go no further than the west of Britain*: D. R. Ragge, *Grasshoppers and Crickets & Cockroaches of the British Isles*, p. 257.

214 *a quarter of Europe's crickets and grasshoppers were at risk of extinction*: see A. Hochkirch et al., *European Red List of Grasshoppers, Crickets and Bush-crickets*. Luxembourg: Publications Office of the European Union, 2016.

214 *nearly half of the world's Orthoptera are now experiencing declines:* Francisco Sánchez-Bayo, 'Worldwide decline of the entomofauna:

A review of its drivers', *Biological Conservation*, vol. 232, April 2019, pp. 8–27.

216 a remarkable act of solidarity occurred: see Tim Tate, *Pride: The Unlikely Story of the True Heroes of the Miner's Strike* (London: John Blake, 2017).

223 *'brain with a twist'*: Samuel Taylor Coleridge, *The Collected Works of Samuel Taylor Coleridge*, vol. 12:1, ed. George Whalley (London: Routledge & Kegan Paul, 1980), p. 796.

Chapter 5: Caves, Pockets, Futures

Pages

227 *'Our excitement grew ... since caves this large were totally unknown'*: Jean-Marie Chauvet, Eliette Brunel Deschamps and Christian Hillaire, *Chauvet Caves: The Discovery of the World's Oldest Paintings* (London: Thames and Hudson, 1996), p. 36.

228 *'We could hardly believe our eyes ... desecrating a sanctuary'*: Jean-Marie Chauvet, Eliette Brunel Deschamps and Christian Hillaire, *Chauvet Caves*, p. 52 and p. 50.

229 *'double energy ... well-thrown rope'*: John Berger, 'Past Present', *Guardian*, 12 October 2002.

230 *96 per cent of mammals on the planet are now livestock, while a mere 4 per cent are wild mammals*: see Yinon M. Bar-On, Rob Phillips and Ron Milo, 'The biomass distribution on Earth', *Proceedings of National Academy of Sciences*, vol. 115, no. 25, June 2018, pp. 6506–511.

230 *'They were for the dark'*: John Berger, 'Past Present'.

230 *For the last 7,000 years, the environmental conditions*: see Dana Nuccitelli, 'New research may resolve a climate 'conundrum' across the history of human civilization', *Guardian*, 14 June 2017.

231 *scores of faunal extinctions*: see Paul L. Koch and Anthony D. Barnosky 'Late Quaternary Extinctions: State of the Debate', *Annual Review of Ecology, Evolution, and Systematics*, vol. 37, no. 1, December 2006, pp. 215–50.

231 *'The pocket in question is a small pocket of resistance'*: John Berger, *The Shape of a Pocket* (London: Bloomsbury, 2001), back cover.

232 *The footprints ... into the cave's depths*: Paul G. Bahn and Jean Vertut, *Journey Through the Ice Age* (London: Seven Dials, 1999), p. 10.

232 *Of particular interest ... held by an adult*: Jean Clottes and David Lewis-Williams, *The Shamans of Prehistory: Trance and Magic in the Painted Caves*, trans. Sophie Hawkes (New York: Harry N. Abrams, 1998), p. 98.

234 *'great gloom ... roof-levelling'*: W. B. Yeats, 'A Prayer for My Daughter' in *The Major Works*, ed. Edward Larrissy (1921; Oxford: Oxford University Press, 2001), p. 32.

Notes

236   *'Everything that does not need you is real'*: W. S. Merwin, 'The Widow' in *Migration: New & Selected Poems* (1966; Port Townsend: Copper Canyon Press, 2005), p. 122.

236   *'ignorance about those who are lost / undermines the reality of the world'*: Zbigniew Herbert, 'Mr Cogito on the Need for Precision' in *The Collected Poems: 1956-1998*, trans. Alissa Valles (1983; New York: Ecco Press, 2008), p. 408. I am grateful to Steven Lovatt for bringing this poem to my attention.

Permissions

Grateful acknowledgement is made to *The Willowherb Review* and to the publishers and editors of *The Gifts of Gravity and Light*, where parts of the 'Eel' chapter appeared before this book was published. Rights to reproduce lyrics by Bob Dylan were granted by Hal Leonard Europe Ltd:

Like A Rolling Stone
Words and Music by Bob Dylan
Copyright © 1965 UNIVERSAL TUNES
Copyright Renewed
All Rights Reserved Used by Permission